D1524066

THE LEVY CAPER

THE LEVY CAPER

by David Shaw

MACMILLAN PUBLISHING CO., INC.
NEW YORK

COLLIER MACMILLAN PUBLISHERS
LONDON

Macmillan Publishing Co., Inc.
866 Third Avenue, New York, N. Y. 10022
Collier-Macmillan Canada Ltd.

Library of Congress Cataloging in Publication Data
Shaw, David, 1943-
     The Levy caper.
     1. Swindlers and swindling—United States. 2. Stocks—United
States. 3. Fraud—United States. I. Title.
HV6695.S5   364.1'63   74-10897
ISBN 0-02-610010-X

First Printing 1974

Printed in the United States of America

*With love for my father
who made it all possible*

Incredible as it may seem at times, what follows is a true story. The names of Alan Levy and most of the other central characters in the story are also genuine. The names of a few peripheral characters have, however, been changed or omitted.

Prologue

I actually got a rather late start in my life of crime," Alan Levy says, almost apologetically. "I was nine years old and I walked into this five-and-dime on Morris Avenue in Chicago, where I grew up, and I stole eight flashlight batteries."

Why did he steal them?

"Because I'm a dumb *schmuck*. I didn't even own a fuckin' flashlight."

That set a pattern Levy has followed throughout his life —stealing and scamming and scheming for the sheer hell of it, for the thrill, the excitement, the challenge of beating the odds, "outsmarting the sharp asses," as he puts it. The money—even as much money as the $800 million he would be after in his big stock swindle—is always incidental for Levy . . . merely the tangible evidence of a well-conceived, well-executed caper.

Levy—all five feet four inches, 180 slightly roly-poly pounds of him—is a character straight out of Damon Runyon . . . by way of Mark Twain. With a mischievous twinkle in his eye, a fat cigar between his teeth and a glib story on his tongue, he is Huck Finn at the Las Vegas crap tables—an incorrigibly puckish, compulsively dishonest, charmingly roguish imp who, somehow, always manages to surround himself with a cast of supporting characters that beggars description and staggers the imagination. Mafiosos, European socialites, bunco artists, FBI agents, international art-swindlers, members of the British aristocracy, punch-drunk prizefighters, hookers, nymphomaniacs —they all seem to filter in and out of Levy's life like flies buzzing around a porch light on a warm midsummer evening.

Levy was a successful bookmaker in Chicago in his early thirties, but—like his father—he was a compulsive gambler, and he lost more money on his own bets than he made on his customers' bets. One day in mid-1963, he tried to recoup his losses by pocketing the money a Syndicate hood gave him to bet on a three-game baseball parlay. Levy has always considered himself something of an expert at handicapping professional sports events—especially baseball and football—and he was convinced there was no way the hood could win his parlay. "Why let him throw the money away?" he reasoned. "I might as well keep it myself, right? He'll never know."

But the hood won his bet—and $8,000. Since Levy didn't even have $800 to pay him with, he suddenly realized how much he'd always wanted to live in California. He borrowed a friend's car and sped to the airport. On the way, in a torrential rainstorm, he rammed into a taxi carrying a pregnant woman.

"Here I was, trying to sneak out of town as quickly and unobtrusively as possible, and I wind up in the middle of a traffic accident, arguing with a cabbie, surrounded by angry, honking drivers and a hysterical pregnant woman."

Any moment, Levy was certain, a big black Cadillac would pull up and two men in dark suits would step out, guns in hand, and he would be a dead man. He panicked.

"I jumped out of the car, left it sitting in the middle of the street and hailed a cab going the other way."

In San Diego, and later in Los Angeles and New York, Levy ran through a succession of legitimate, semi-legitimate and downright illegitimate businesses—bookmaking, swindling, running a bar, owning a couple of dress stores, managing a prizefighter, selling luggage and pillows. He also ran through a succession of wives—six altogether. His compulsive gambling on sports events destroyed his businesses and his marriages; his losses ate up his profits, and the resultant tensions and pressures drove away his wives.

Levy had an encounter or two with the law during this period, too, the most serious coming when he was arrested for bookmaking in Los Angeles in 1964. "I didn't know shit about L.A. then," he says. "I'd just gotten back to town from the East, and I got me a black suit and black shirt and white tie, and I started driving around in a big, white Caddy. It was like I was carrying a sign. I should've put an ad in *The Times:* 'Make book here.' The cops were putting the heat on all the stoolies then, and every stoolie in town needed someone to turn in to keep the cops off their backs; so they all turned me in. Guys I didn't even know turned me in. I was everyone's favorite patsy. I'd only been back in L.A. about three months when I got busted, but the cops made it look like I ran the biggest book west of the Mississippi. Fortunately, the judge slept through my trial, and I only got a two-hundred-dollar fine. I told the judge I didn't have the money, and he said I could pay it on time. Wonderful."

Levy continued to bet—and lose—heavily, and late in the 1969 football season he lost $48,000 in one weekend to a bookmaker known locally as "Marty the Nose." When Levy lost to a bookmaker, he usually either paid him off out of previous winnings or—more often, since winnings were scarce—he just refused to pay at all. "You're stiffed," he'd say, and in Los Angeles, where there is not the threat of organized crime reprisals that exists in cities like New York and Chicago and Miami, he would generally get away with it. But Levy considers Marty a friend, not just another bookie, and he never stiffs a friend if he can possibly avoid it; when he couldn't pay a penny of the $48,-000 he lost to Marty, he became despondent.

In an attempt to earn money to pay off his losses, Levy started his own sports forecasting network—a mail and telephone tout service providing inside information to other bettors. Like most of his business ventures, it was immediately successful. But, as always, Levy's own gambling losses far outstripped his business income, and he was soon further in the hole than ever. In a matter of weeks, he lost $3,000 to a bookie in Fort Wayne, $6,000 to a bookie in Philadelphia, $12,000 to a bookie in Portland and $18,000 to a bookie in Atlanta. Unable to pay any of them, he was living on the knife-edge of disaster—broke, bored, restive, looking over his shoulder for his creditors, losing interest in his sports forecasting service, increasingly apprehensive that the bookies just might decide to join forces and come looking for him. . . .

Chapter 1

It all began—as so many misadventures seem to begin—amid feelings of despair, desperation and a general malaise that can only be characterized as "What-have-I-got-to-lose?" Out of work, deeply in debt to bookmakers and loan sharks, struggling to support his sixth wife and nine-month-old daughter, his fertile hustler's mind strangely barren of get-rich-quick schemes, Alan Levy was ripe for virtually any enterprise that promised money and excitement, no matter how risky or outlandish.

In early February, 1971, just such an enterprise was dumped in Levy's ample lap.

Levy had fallen four months behind in his rent on a swank penthouse apartment by then, and he and his wife and daughter had moved to a rented home in the West Los Angeles suburb of Cheviot Hills. Money had become so scarce in the Levy household that the telephone had been disconnected. He was doing his "business" on a pay phone at a private tennis club across the street.

"We had an eight-hundred-dollar phone bill," Levy recalls. "Most of it was for my calls to bookies."

Not that the discontinuance of telephone service—or the family's precarious financial plight—had put an end to Levy's gambling. Only death could do that—and even then, Levy always said, "If there ain't no bookies in heaven, then it ain't heaven, and I ain't goin'."

He had just experienced a particularly disastrous betting weekend, in fact, losing more than $7,000—$7,000 he didn't have, of course—on college and professional football games. The college games, on Saturday, had cost him about $1,-800. The pro games, on Sunday, had been worse. The crusher had come Monday night in ABC's weekly Howard Cosell/Don Meredith "Can-you-top-this?" bowl. Levy had blown $2,000 on that one game—the one game that whole week he had been certain he'd win . . . "an absolute lock," he'd assured everyone who subscribed to his sports forecasting service. ("That," he later realized, "was one of my big problems—I believed all my own bullshit. I actually thought I knew what I was talking about with all those *cockamamy* predictions.")

On Tuesday night, wallowing in self-pity and wearing only his baggy boxer shorts and sagging brown socks, Levy lay on the living room floor, watching television. About seven o'clock, an old friend named Steve Berg dropped by. Levy had once dated—and employed—the woman who was now Berg's wife, and the two men had become good friends in recent years. Berg ran an industrial linen supply company in East Los Angeles, and his family was prominent in both banking and the scrap paper and rag business. Berg was thirty-two then, with rapidly thinning, reddish-brown hair, blue eyes and—almost invariably—a suit and tie. But this evening, his shirt was open at the neck, his tie was askew and he seemed flushed and fidgety.

"I've got a sensational deal," Berg told Levy in a hoarse whisper he didn't want Mrs. Levy to overhear.

Levy didn't even ask for details. He skipped dinner, said goodbye to his wife and left with Berg.

"In the mood I was in," he recalls, "I wouldn't give a shit if it was robbing banks. I just had to get money. Besides, I knew it wouldn't be robbing banks. Steve was a very straight kind of guy, completely honest. Like a lot of straight guys, he probably would have liked to be a crook. He was really fascinated with that way of life. But he didn't know how, really."

When they got into Berg's car, Levy asked where they were going.

"East Los Angeles. Not far from my office."

"Oh."

As they drove, Berg picked up his car telephone.

"Remember the guy I told you about?" he said to someone on the other end. "The guy with all the underworld connections who's gonna help us with that stuff you got? Well, I'm bringing him over now. Make sure you're at the plant. We don't want to drive all the way over there from Cheviot Hills on a wild goose chase. Have some of the stuff ready, too, Gerry. He's gonna want to take a good look at it."

Levy stared at Berg incredulously, his mouth agape.

"It was obvious he was talking to whoever his *farkokte* contact was in East Los Angeles, and they had some shady deal going, and here's Steve yapping over his car phone like nobody's listening. Those kind of phones have eleven, twelve channels. Everyone and his mother spends time listening to everyone else, and here's Steve shooting his mouth off about 'underworld connections' and calling the guy by his right name and telling the world I live in Cheviot Hills. He might as well have published all our addresses and telephone numbers in the *FBI Bulletin*, for Christ's sake. I was dealing with a couple of real pros; I could see that right away."

When Berg hung up, Levy asked, "You gonna tell me what the hell this whole *megillah's* about, or we going to some kind of surprise birthday party for the Pope?"

Berg, rattled, said he didn't know too many details, "but a guy I do business with has some stocks and bonds. A lot of them. He isn't sure what to do with them, so he asked me, and I don't know either. I figured you would."

"Me? What I know about stocks and bonds you can put

in your *pupick*. You need cash to buy stocks and bonds. You ever see me with cash?"

Berg grinned.

"No, but you seem to know your way around pretty good, and with your contacts and all. . . . Look, I told the guy you really knew what you were doing. There's millions of dollars here, and you're supposed to be a sophisticated stock manipulator and . . ."

Levy interrupted him. "Millions?" His voice was more skeptical than awed, but even as he spoke the magic word, his adrenalin began to pump and the cash registers—no, the slot machines—began to flicker in his eyes. Berg's uncle, he knew, was a successful banker, a man who had undoubtedly forgotten more about stocks and bonds than Alan Levy would ever know. Steve should have gone to his uncle, not him, with this deal—unless. . . . Sure, that was it. The deal definitely must be a little shady. More than a little. Levy waggled his cigar and peered out the car window into the dark night. Things were looking up. Yes, indeed. Things were looking up.

The two men were silent, each thinking his own quiet thoughts, as Berg pulled on to the Santa Monica Freeway, one of more than a dozen major superhighways that crisscross the Los Angeles basin like tourniquets hastily applied to the victim of massive hemorrhaging. They drove east on the freeway, through West Los Angeles and downtown and then into East Los Angeles, the city's largest Mexican-American *barrio*. More Mexicans live in Los Angeles than in any other city in the world except Mexico City itself, and their largest single concentration—almost 200,000 people—is in East Los Angeles, a crowded, teeming collection of ramshackle homes, tiny mom-and-pop grocery stores and garishly neoned bars, pool halls and cut-rate furniture stores. East Los Angeles—East L.A.—is precisely where its name implies: just east of downtown L.A. It was one of the few areas of the city Levy was unfamiliar with, and as

Berg raced off the freeway and on to Eastern Avenue, one of the main north-south streets in the *barrio*, Levy glanced briefly at the surroundings, puffed on his cigar, and said, "Aw right, where the hell you taking me?"

Berg's answer was to pull his long, brown Buick Riviera up a wide black-top driveway in front of a green cement-block building less than a mile off the freeway. A large sign identified the dilapidated-looking building as the Kassap Rag Company. Berg ushered Levy inside, and introduced him to Gerry Kassap, the vice-president. Kassap—40 years old, his heavy belly protruding over his belt, his face naturally oily, his hands unnaturally dirty, "a real *zhlub*" in Levy's words—seemed very impressed with himself, despite his appearance and surroundings.

The office Kassap was standing in was small and cramped, with two desks and very little light, and he quickly escorted Levy and Berg out of the office into the plant itself, where the floors were littered with multicolored scraps of rag and paper. "It was a scroungy, sweaty place," Levy says. "Kassap brought bits and pieces of rags and paper there and shredded it and baled it up and sold it. That was his whole business."

As Kassap guided Levy and Berg through the plant out to his loading platform, three large dogs approached them. Levy walked toward one. The dog growled and jumped him—"damn near knocked me down."

Millions of dollars or not, Levy was thinking less and less of this operation every moment.

"It was dark and smelly and dirty, like a scummy old warehouse. I was going to make a million dollars here? Bullshit! I was ready to go home. But thanks to Steve, I had already psyched myself into thinking I was a half-assed stock manipulator. Millions of dollars? Hell, I had already mentally spent my share, and I was busy trying to figure out how to screw those guys out of their end of the deal. Only I didn't know what the deal was yet."

Kassap took Levy and Berg into a dank, dimly-lit room, and pointed to four large barrels. When Levy grumbled about the darkness, Kassap flicked on an overhead light. Then he began lifting large sheets of parchment-like paper out of the barrels. Some of them were municipal bonds. Levy didn't recognize those at first. But for all his ignorance of the stock market, he had seen a stock certificate or two in his time. At least, he had a pretty good idea what one was when he saw it. And he saw hundreds of thousands of them in the barrels. They were in long, uncut sheets, rolled up and stuffed in like trash. In other barrels, Kassap showed him department-store gift certificates and blank corporate payroll checks and dividend checks and check-cashing cards from major commercial banks.

"He had stacks and stacks and stacks of this stuff. Reams of it. I thought, what is this? It looks like we're gonna play Monopoly. He had rolls of Bank of America check-cashing cards—the plain paper, before they're laminated in plastic. Rolls! It was like toilet paper. And the stock certificates—Jesus, some of the most solid companies around—IBM, Walt Disney Studios, TWA, Western Airlines, Times-Mirror, Mattel Toys, Carnation Milk, TraveLodge Motels, Lear-Siegler, Anheuser-Busch, a couple of banks, a big life insurance company or two. Unbelievable. We were all gonna be millionaires. Zillionaires. Overnight. Overnight? Hell, why wait overnight. Right now. This minute. I was already retiring."

Levy, trying to sound knowledgeable but not too excited, asked Kassap how he came into possession of such a windfall. Kassap said he did business with a paper-shredder in northern California, near San Francisco, and the paper-shredder was occasionally called upon to destroy unissued stock certificates, municipal bonds and the like. The material would be overruns, outdated items, slightly imperfect issues or otherwise invalid securities (which would, nevertheless, appear perfectly legitimate to all but the most trained eye).

Kassap said he had been in the shredder's plant one day recently when two Brinks armored trucks delivered a shipment of these securities from the "Jeffries Banknote Company of San Francisco." The entire contents of the shipment were to be destroyed, and the Brinks guards, Kassap told Levy, were supposed to witness the destruction process themselves so their records could properly reflect the completion of the process. But on this particular afternoon, the shredder's telephone rang before he could finish loading his shredder/grinder, and the guards didn't want to wait around until he was through talking, so they signed all the papers and left. Or so Kassap said. The shredder— Levy can't remember if his name was Herman or Sherman "or maybe it was *Shmendrick*, for all I know"—then went to answer the telephone, leaving Kassap alone in the room with half the Brinks shipment lying on the floor. Kassap said he had gone to the plant to pick up several large bales of shredded paper to take to his own plant in East Los Angeles, and—as he told the story to Levy—his shredder-friend gestured toward several such bales on his way to the telephone and told Kassap "Pick out the ones you want us to ship down to L.A. for you."

"Gerry," says Levy, "doesn't know from nothin' about stock certificates, but he's bright enough to figure out that anything surrounded by armed Brinks guards must be valuable, right? So he starts frantically pushing the stock certificates and bonds and everything else into the bales of chopped-up paper. When his friend comes back, he's got the bales loaded with stock certificates, and he casually points to those bales—"I'll take that one and that one and those three and that one over there"—as the ones to be shipped to his plant in East Los Angeles. When the shipment arrived, Gerry told me, he didn't even let his employees open them. 'I cut them open myself,' he said. 'I took out the stock certificates and bonds and everything and put them in those barrels. There they are.'

"Sounds logical, right? You want to see what an idiot I

am? First of all, I believe the *schmuck* when he says Jeffries Banknote Company is in San Francisco. Jeffries Banknote Company is visible from the Harbor Freeway just south of downtown Los Angeles on the way to the Los Angeles Coliseum, where I've only seen like eight thousand football games over the years. But, what the hell, maybe they have offices in San Francisco, too, right? But I also believed that bullshit about stuffing millions and millions of dollars worth of huge stock certificates into bales of chopped-up paper. You ever see a bale? It's like a cotton bale or hay bale. They're packed so tight you can't pull one shred out with tweezers and pliers. And Gerry's supposed to be forcing certificates in by the thousand—without tearing them or dirtying them or wrinkling them. And he does all this while the guy's on one phone call. Who's he talking to—his grandmother who he hasn't seen since Poland in 1928? I mean even if he could stuff all those certificates in the bales, it would take him six hundred and eighty-four years to do it, right? But that doesn't faze me. He keeps telling the story, and I keep nodding. Like an idiot. Now, really, I got to be a mental case. The dumbest thing of all, though, is I don't even ask what he was supposed to do with all the shredded paper. I mean, Gerry's a paper-shredder, too. What the hell does a paper-shredder go to San Francisco to get already shredded paper for? It's like a barber filling his shop with a bunch of guys who just got their hair cut somewhere else. What's he gonna do? Sit back and criticize the other guy's work? That and thirty-five cents will get him a subway ride. But I'm not thinking like that. All I know is I need some bread and Gerry's got enough stuff to make me more bread than I ever dreamed of. He could tell me four green men brought the stuff from Mars in a flying saucer and I'd have believed him."

It didn't occur to Levy until much later that Kassap himself was the "northern California" shredder who had originally been given all the stock certificates and other material for destruction. The material had indeed come from Jeffries Banknote Company—in Los Angeles. All told, there was $800 million worth of securities there. Each company represented in the securities probably had a slightly different reason for wanting the items destroyed, but, in essence, the circumstances were basically the same. The largest single parcel of stock certificates, for example, belonged to the International Chemical and Nuclear Corporation.* There were 1,529 certificates of 100 shares each, 220 certificates for less than 100 shares each (the exact number of shares was not filled in) and 251 certificates for unlimited numbers of shares—tens of millions of dollars' worth of stock certificates for a very reputable company whose stock was then selling at about $50 a share.

So why were the certificates being destroyed?

In July 1970, International Chemical and Nuclear Corp. had gained a coveted listing on the New York Stock Exchange. Previously, it had been listed on the American Stock Exchange. Because of the new listing, company officials decided to issue new stock certificates, bearing the new listing, a different design and the signatures of a new registrar and transfer agent. That meant the old certificates—technically, unissued shares of stock—had to be destroyed. Since the Jeffries Banknote Company had helped prepare the new certificates, they were asked to see to the destruction of the old ones. On December 23, 1970, the old stock certificates had been shipped to Jeffries by railway express from Chase Manhattan Bank in New York, then the transfer agent for International Chemical and Nuclear Corp. On December 28, the shipment arrived in Los Angeles.

In years past, such certificates had been incinerated—"burned to ashes," in the words of the formal instructions that always accompanied the shipments. But the high rag content of these particular certificates—combined with anti-

---

* Today, this company is called ICN Pharmaceutical.

pollution ordinances prohibiting most refuse incineration in the city of Los Angeles—made it necessary for Jeffries to seek an alternative means of destruction.

On January 21, the certificates were placed in six large metal "destruction bins." On February 1, representatives of Certified Incinerator Company picked them up and, very shortly thereafter, delivered them to the Kassap Rag Company in East Los Angeles for shredding and grinding. Larry Gamson of Certified Incinerator Company—presumably one of the "Brinks guards" in Kassap's story to Levy—signed the necessary destruction forms, which said:

"We, the undersigned, hereby certify that the above number of containers were picked up on this date and removed to plant for destruction via grinder. All precautions were taken to ensure security by immediate destruction of all contents."

Except, of course, that the contents were not destroyed. Kassap had them, and he had called Berg, a business associate whose family was also in the paper business, to see what might be done with them. Kassap thought Berg was probably the brightest, best-connected man he knew. Berg felt the same way about Alan Levy. For years, he had heard Levy talking about big-money deals, sleight-of-hand scams and his connections with "the big boys"—presumably organized crime figures in Los Angeles and his native Chicago.

So here they were—Levy, Berg and Kassap—at nine o'clock on a Tuesday night, poring over $800 million worth of valuable securities in an East Los Angeles paper-shredding plant . . . about as unlikely a location, and even more unlikely a trio, as ever became involved in what was, potentially, the biggest stock swindle in American history.

Eight hundred million dollars. Almost a billion dollars. Levy savored the sound and smell and taste of it: O-N-E B-I-L-L-I-O-N   D-O-L-L-A-R-S . . . . For a small-time hustler who had spent his whole lifetime wandering greedily around the fringes of big money, it was an altogether staggering figure to grasp—a heart-numbing, stomach-churning, mind-boggling figure. Laid end-to-end, in $1 bills, it would stretch from Levy's home to London and back *nine* times. Hell, it would stretch around the whole damn world five times! Even in nice, crisp $100 bills, it would stretch from Chicago to Boston. And it was all in negotiable securities—nothing stolen, nothing counterfeit, nothing listed with any law enforcement agency. Everything 100 percent legitimate—except, of course, that none of it really belonged to Alan Levy . . . or to anyone else, for that matter . . . .

Chapter 2

Alan Levy didn't know much more than Gerry Kassap or Steve Berg did about what could be done with the gold mine he'd stumbled on. But he wasn't about to let his ignorance show. He sorted through the material, nodding and mumbling knowingly from time to time, and all the while trying to decide where to go for advice.

"I knew I was going to be rich from this," he says. "I just didn't know who else I'd have to cut in."

When he'd made a casual survey of the contents of the barrels, he looked up at Berg and Kassap, both hovering nearby, awaiting the words that would make them all instant millionaires. Levy manufactured his fiercest glare and warned them:

"We could all go to jail for this stuff, you know."

They nodded dumbly.

He was clearly in command.

"Okay, look, have you talked to anyone else about this?"

Berg looked at Kassap. Kassap shook his head.

Only the fat cigar clenched between his teeth kept Levy from breaking into a grin of smug triumph. "Good," he told them. "Don't. No one. And I mean no one. Unless you two want to spend the rest of your lives in jail some place. Don't get greedy. Don't try to get someone else to handle the stock for you, too. I'll handle the whole thing. Understand?"

Kassap said he did.

"Okay," Levy said. "Talk to you in a few days. Let's get out of here, Steve."

With that, Levy purposefully scooped up a few samples of "the merchandise"—the code word he insisted Berg and Kassap use henceforth—and Berg drove him home to Cheviot Hills. Neither man said much on the way. Berg had been so frightened by Levy's intimations of imprisonment that he was even afraid to talk to Levy! Levy, meanwhile, was too busy thinking to talk. He was trying to decide to whom he should take the samples, how big a cut he'd have to give them, how much he'd have to give Berg and Kassap —and what prison he'd like to spend his time in when they were ultimately caught.

"From the very beginning, that first night, I never expected to get away with it all the way. I knew, sooner or later, either Freddie, Bernie and Irving (Levy's euphemism for the FBI) or Izzie, Ronald and Sam (the IRS) would catch up to us. The only question was how much money could I salt away before then. I looked at it this way— suppose, out of all that eight hundred million dollars, I only managed to salvage eighty million. That seemed pretty conservative then, right? I mean a return of only ten percent on that big a killing. A cinch, right? Well, I figured the worst I could get if we got busted was a nickel—five years in the joint. With time off for good behavior and all that shit, I'd actually serve about forty months—a little better than three years. That figured out to about twenty-five million dollars a year, tax-free, the way I calculated riding home with Steve that night. Not a bad salary. I'd go to the joint for those wages any day. Hell, even if the whole deal fell apart around my ears and I only made two hundred fifty thousand dollars—mere pennies, right?— that would be eighty-five thousand dollars a year. Still not exactly starvation wages. I could come out of the joint and live happily ever after on that. And I knew, just knew, we were talking about a lot more dough than that. That's the way my mind was working that night. I knew I was no master criminal who was gonna fool the world. Master criminal? Hah, the Hansel and Gretel of criminals was more like it. I wasn't kidding myself. I was just figuring the odds, and for that kind of money, the odds looked pretty fuckin' good that night. Besides, it wasn't just the money. It never was with me. It was the risk, the excitement, the whole feeling you get from a good scam."

For several days after the first meeting with Kassap and Berg, Levy tried to figure the angles. Uppermost in his mind was finding an advisor with several important qualifications:

"He had to know all about stocks and bonds, of course. He had to be greedy enough to want to help out in exchange for a small piece of the action, rather than run straight to the cops. And he had to have balls. If things got a little hairy, I didn't want some partner who got tobacco stains in his underwear every time someone walked by who looked like a cop."

Finally, Levy called Jack Lane, a realtor he knew who had put together a number of real estate deals and was supposed to have banking connections in the Bahamas. Levy wasn't altogether certain Lane knew as much about the stock and bond market as he did about real estate, but he was sure Lane could put him in touch with the right people if he didn't know himself. More important, at this stage, Levy felt he could trust Lane; the two had been so close that Levy had often given Lane some of his clothes when styles—or Levy's fickle tastes—had changed.

When he called Lane on the telephone from the tennis club across the street—"my executive offices, very professional and big-time"—Levy was deliberately vague about the exact nature of the transaction he had in mind.

"I'm paranoid," he admits. "When you're always scamming, you get that way. You figure every phone you use is tapped and every guy who walks on the same street as you for more than a block is a tail from Interpol."

All Levy told Lane was that he had "a very big deal in the works," involving the stock market, and he wanted Lane to "look at a couple of things and give me some advice." They made an appointment for eight o'clock Wednesday night.

Levy was driving an orange Fiat Spider then—"of course, that was only temporary; I practically had my Rolls on order already"—and at the appointed hour Wednesday night, he made the ten-minute 'rive from his home to Lane's office on La Cienega Boulevard in West Los Angeles. The stretch of La Cienega on which Lane's office was located is known locally as Restaurant Row. Some of the more expensive, but not necessarily the best, restaurants in Los Angeles are spread along both sides of eight blocks on La Cienega, from Wilshire Boulevard north to Melrose Avenue. But Lane's office didn't seem to fit in these lush environs. It was a small office, above one of Levy's old dress shops and next door to his old sports forecasting service. There were two "suites" in the office—"if they were suites," Levy says, "then I'm Calvin Coolidge"—one with two desks and three chairs, the other with a bed.

Levy had gone to the neighborhood drugstore earlier in the day to buy a briefcase to carry the stock samples in— "I bought the best one they had . . . two dollars and ninety-eight cents"—and he lost no time setting it on one of the desks, opening it and showing Lane the merchandise.

"He took one look at it and knew it was the real thing," he says. "I only had maybe two hundred dollars' worth with me, and he wanted to know how I got it and how much more I could get. I mean, it was pretty obvious to him that I wouldn't have come looking for his advice if I'd bought the stuff normal-like from my friendly neighborhood stockbroker."

Levy told Lane the whole story, and when he was

through, Lane suggested calling a broker/friend who had worked for a prominent Beverly Hills bond house, and was now in insurance and real estate. He could tell them all what to do next, Lane said.

"I liked him the minute he told me his name—H. Cabot Jones. Does that sound like class? H. Cabot Jones. He probably had his own yacht and a chauffeur, right? Well, it was 9:30 or so by then, and Jack calls him and tells him to come right over. Jones must have thought it was an emergency or something because he was there in nothing flat, still wearing his pajamas, with a topcoat over them."

Jones was five foot eleven, 150 pounds, bespectacled, gray-haired, slightly stoop-shouldered and hard-of-hearing. He looked, in Levy's words, "like sixty-two going on eighty." As Levy later learned, when Jones donned one of his English-cut suits and a white shirt and tie, he cut an imposing figure indeed . . . suave, distinguished, sophisticated, respectable. "But if you put a pair of overalls on him and stuck him on Skid Row, everyone who passed by would give him a dime for a cup of coffee." That night—in his topcoat, with his pajamas protruding from his sleeves and pants legs—he looked more the bum than the banker.

"He sounded like he knew what he was talking about, though. He told us the stock was legitimate, and he gave a little speech on how the stock market works, and it sounded like we had a real expert on our hands. Then I told him how I got the stock.

"What do you think I should do with it," I asked him.

"Burn it."

"Burn it? What do you mean burn it? There's millions and millions of dollars here. Since when do I need an expert's advice to burn it? I can think of that bright idea myself."

Jones said that if they were determined to trade the securities, they should concentrate on the stock itself, at least in the beginning. It would probably offer less risk and greater return than the bonds, charge cards, bank cards, gift certificates and all.

"He said we should forget about trading it through normal brokerage channels. Since the stock had never been officially issued, it wouldn't be registered with transfer agents—whatever the hell they were—and we'd get caught before any money was disbursed. Our best bet, he said, might be to use the stock as collateral for big bank loans. That way, no one would bother to check the stock with transfer agents. It would just sit in the bank vault until we paid off the loan. Then we could get it back and do the same thing all over again. In the meantime, we'd be able to use the money we borrowed to make low-risk investments.

"I didn't much like the sound of that at first, but like I said, Jones really seemed to know what he was talking about, so I got to thinking. First, of course, there was no way I was going to pay any bank loans back. Forget that, Charley. They were stiffed. Automatic. One of my first rules of life is: 'If you borrow cash, you don't pay back.' Once I ask you to lend me five dollars, don't talk to me any more. I don't borrow to pay back. And if I do pay back, it's not in cash. It's by check. And if the check is any good, you are the luckiest person in the world. So if you loan me any money, you should right away make an appointment with a psychiatrist."

So Levy decided that using the stock for loan collateral wasn't such a bad idea if you had no intention of ever repaying the loan. In fact, he thought, why even bother with the "low-risk investments" Jones spoke of? Why waste time getting 8 or 10 percent on, say, $1 million, when you could use that same time and energy to take more stock and make another $1 million loan? Besides, by the time the bank realized the loan wasn't going to be paid back—and that the stock they had taken as collateral was no good—

Levy figured to have the money spent or socked safely away.

Levy asked what kind of loan they could get on the stock—"how much dough?"—and was told "anywhere from sixty to eighty percent of face value of the stock, depending on the economic climate and the credit of the man applying for the loan."

None of those present had financial statements that would warrant six- or seven-figure loans, but Jones said he knew a man who might be able to help them. Of course, the man would make the loan himself and be obligated to pay it back; since he was taking the risk, he would probably only pay Levy and his partners a small percentage of the face value of the stock.

"How small?" Levy asked.

"Maybe ten cents on the dollar."

Again, Levy's first reaction was negative—to put it mildly. He had originally hoped to sell all the stock at face value. Then Jones had told him he might have to settle for 60 to 80 percent of face value in the form of a loan. Now Jones was saying he might net only 10 percent of face value.

"But I'm really not greedy," Levy insists. "Hell, ten cents on the dollar, with eight hundred million dollars at stake, was still eighty million dollars. For eighty million, I could afford to be generous with this other guy—whoever he was —and take just ten percent for myself."

Levy asked Jones who he had in mind for the deal.

The man's name was Rod, Jones said, and he divided his time among New York, Montreal, Vancouver and the Bahamas. His wife held a seat on one of the major stock exchanges, he had some kind of off-shore mutual fund and he had dealings in the international money market. Levy might want to dump the stock abroad, Jones said, and this man would know the proper way to do it.

"I probably should have asked him right there why I'd

want to dump it abroad," Levy says, "but I was getting
dizzy by then.

"You have to picture this scene. Here I got a chance for
a big score—a *big* score. So who gets me involved? A friend
who thinks he's Walter Mitty and a rag-picker from East
L.A. Okay, so I take the deal to a pro, and he has an office that looks like it belongs to an out-of-work Fuller
Brush man, and he calls in a half-ass expert who's half-
deaf, comes to our meeting in pajamas and tells me to
burn everything. But he tells me he's got some kind of
cockamamy friend in Saskatchewan or some *farkokte* place
with a big-deal wife and an off-shore mutual fund, which,
for all I know about the stock market, means an oil well
in the middle of the Red Sea.

"Now all the while the three of us are holding our meeting, some guy I never saw before keeps barging in, looking
around, saying, 'Oh, excuse me, am I interrupting something?' and running back out again. A half a dozen times,
at least, he does that. He's a guy in his mid-forties, I guess,
very Irish-looking, with rheumy eyes, like a guy who drinks
too much. And he's got ears that stick out like an elephant's.
Finally, I ask Jack what the fuck the guy thinks he's doing,
and Jack says, 'He's Fred Ryan. You know that office next
door? The one with the bed? Well, he and his wife live
there.'

"I couldn't believe it. 'They what?' He said it again:
'They live there.' I exploded. 'Live there? In that hole?
I thought this was an office, a business office, you know,
with desks and typewriters and files. You mean they actually sleep in there?' " Lane nodded.

"Anyway, through all this confusion, I'm trying to make
a multimillion-dollar deal. Wonderful. Just wonderful. But
I tell Jones I like the sound of this friend of his. 'Why
don't we call him?' Jones says he thinks he's in Montreal.
'So?' I ask him. 'They don't have telephones in Montreal?'
Jones looks at his watch and says, 'It's almost eleven o'clock.

That means it's two o'clock in the morning in Montreal."

Levy muttered something about "an expert who can show me how to tell time I don't need," then suggested calling anyway:

"I don't even know the guy, but for this kind of money, I guarantee you he won't mind interrupting his beauty sleep." Levy was right. But Jones was very circumspect over the telephone. He had never been involved in anything even remotely shady before, and at this stage in his life, he wasn't exactly thrilled by the prospect of a scandal and a prison sentence. He just told his friend Rod that some business associates had a deal he might be interested in, and it would require his physical presence to examine a few documents.

Rod told Jones he was leaving the next day for New York, and then had to make a quick trip to the Bahamas. Jones gave him his telephone number and Lane's office number. When Rod returned to Montreal, he said, he'd call Jones or Lane and arrange to fly out to Los Angeles to look at "the merchandise," as Jones, too, was now calling the stock.

That's how everyone left things that night: Rod would call Jones or Lane, and one of them (or Ryan) would then contact Levy to arrange the next meeting.

"You can see already what an airtight deal this is going to be, right? I mean, I'm in it two days, and already I got six partners. But I still don't have a phone. Jack or one of them would have to come to my house."

The next day, Levy walked over to the tennis club to call Steve Berg. He still laughs over the situation he found himself in—"millions of dollars at stake, a big international swindle, and I'm bumming dimes off a guy in tennis shorts so I can call my illustrious partners in crime."

Levy didn't really want to go back through Berg to Kassap, but he didn't know where Kassap lived, and he couldn't remember where his plant was. In fact, to this day, Levy says he couldn't find the plant if he had "two maps, a team of bloodhounds, a flashlight and Sherlock Holmes himself." So he called Berg.

"I got a guy who's interested in the merchandise," he told him. "I need more of it, lots more." Levy wanted to be more specific, but he realized he and Berg had neglected to devise an elaborate code for referring to the various kinds of securities involved. "Shit!" he said aloud. Then, in a style utterly befitting the Grade-B spy movie he was beginning to feel very much a part of, he glanced surreptitiously around the tennis club lobby. The only other man in the building was reading a newspaper. Levy cupped his right hand over the phone and started whispering:

"All I want right now is the stock. The bonds and the Bank of America cards rolled like toilet paper I'm not interested in yet. Look at the stock carefully, though. If I remember correctly, some of it's numbered and some of it isn't. The numbered stuff looks more finished, more legitimate. Let's start with that. Bring me over a few million dollars' worth." Levy liked the sound of that—the way he said "a few million dollars' worth." So casual. So matter-of-fact. Already he was feeling better. Berg suggested they meet at his office in a couple of days. In the meantime, he would see Kassap and make a formal inventory of all the stock. Levy said that was just fine and he once more cautioned Berg against discussing the stock with anyone.

"Tell Kassap that, too," he said. "I don't want him shopping this stuff around. We ain't Macy's or Safeway, tell him. I want aʳ exclusive on this, or I'm getting out. The more people that know about it, you can forget getting rich. We'll all be in jail before the banks open tomorrow. Remember: no shopping around. You shop the stuff with Herman, Sherman and *Shmendrick,* and before you know it, your customers are Freddie, Bernie and Irving."

Berg assured Levy he'd convey his warnings to Kassap. But he was already too late.

The next day, Levy heard "on the street"—that informal

but astonishingly efficient communications network that always seems to exist among those trying to stay one step ahead of the law—that Kassap had approached at least one other person with the stock. Fortunately, Levy had previously met the man through his sports forecasting service. The man was a big gambler who'd been involved in bribing scores of college basketball players to fix games. Levy called him. The man came to his house. They didn't talk long—just long enough for Levy to lay first claim to the stock, minimize its actual market value and greatly exaggerate (or so he thought at the time) the difficulties involved in converting the stock to spendable cash. Stock manipulation really wasn't the other man's game anyway, so—with a handshake and a "good luck" wish—he told Levy he'd bow out of the deal.

Levy went back to the tennis club to call Berg.

"I wanna see Kassap. Fast. Don't ask me why."

Berg called Kassap to arrange the meeting, then drove to Cheviot Hills to pick up Levy. On the drive to East Los Angeles, he tried only once to ask Levy what he wanted to see Kassap about. Levy's response—"Shut your mouth, and drive the car"—silenced him. When they pulled to a stop in front of Kassap's plant, Levy didn't even wait for Berg to shut the ignition off. He bounded from the car with remarkable speed and agility for a man his size, strode through the front door of the plant and shouted to no one in particular, "Where's Kassap?"

Kassap shuffled over.

Levy glared at him for a minute, trying to decide how best to proceed. He had originally planned to greet Kassap with an outright accusation that he had offered the stock to someone else in violation of their agreement. But now he was having second thoughts. Maybe he should give Kassap a chance to volunteer the information first. Maybe he would have a reasonable explanation. After all, they were going to be partners. No sense alienating him so soon.

"You haven't tried to shop the merchandise with anyone else, have you?" he asked Kassap.

Kassap said he had not.

Levy remembers thinking to himself: "Great! Right off the bat, I know my partner is a liar and a cheat. I'm really set. One of my original partners is a liar and a cheat, and the other guy is a half-assed would-be criminal who isn't even sure he really wants to be a criminal. Between the three stooges here we're going to take a shot at beating the FBI, the IRS, Interpol and God knows who else. We're out on the yellow brick road to Oz. Sensational."

Levy's resolve to remain calm quickly evaporated. He stood nose-to-nose with Kassap, threatening him with everything from torture to a Mafia-style execution ("I got a guy'll dump you in the Pacific Ocean with your head in a block of cement") if he approached anyone else with the stock.

Under most circumstances, Levy is like an affection-starved puppy; elfin, roly-poly, puffing on that comic-strip cigar, he's about as intimidating as Julie Andrews. But when he's mad—and particularly when he's mad on the telephone, where you can't see the belly or the cigar or the twinkling eyes—he can be menace and mayhem incarnate. His voice an ugly snarl, the air blue with profanity, the threats of violence coming at you like .45-caliber bullets, he can leave even the biggest and most confident of men shaken, weak-kneed hulks.

That's the treatment he turned on Kassap—nasty, vicious, terrifying. As the original "owner" of the stock, Kassap had initially hoped to keep most of the proceeds for himself. But by the time Levy had finished with him in his office that day, he was more than willing to accept an equal three-way split with Levy and Berg.

"At least, that's what he thought he was going to get," Levy says. "I knew these guys would never know what kind of deal actually went down, though. I mean, when I would get through telling them about the collateral and the financial statements and the ten cents on the dollar, they wouldn't know which end was up. When the time came, I'd give them enough to keep them happy and I'd pocket the rest. After all, I was doing all the work."

Before they concluded that conversation, Levy and Kassap agreed that Berg would come to Kassap's plant to make a full inventory of the stock—and Kassap once more swore, "on his mother's grave this time," not to breathe a word of the deal to another soul.

Did Levy believe him?

"I'm not that big an idiot."

A couple of days later, Levy went to Berg's office in East Los Angeles to examine the inventory he'd drawn up.

He laughs.

"Steven not only had an inventory, he was carrying the *Wall Street Journal*, and he was busy looking up what our stock was worth. Every time I saw him after that, it was the same thing. He always had the *Wall Street Journal*, and he'd always shove a stock table in my face and tell me this stock we had went up four points and this one went up two-and-a-half, and we'd made this much profit and—like a regular stockbroker he was already. To hear him talk, we actually owned all the stock legal-like, and whenever we wanted, we could call our broker and say, 'Okay, Marvin, sell fifty thousand shares of International Chemical and Nuclear, and use that money to buy me some AT&T and General Motors. When that goes up six points, sell it. Don't bother calling me for approval; I'll be in Saint-Tropez all spring."

When Levy and Berg finished examining the inventory, Berg suggested Levy pick up the stock from Kassap himself.

But Levy was feeling pretty important by then, and he was tired of running around to meetings and telephone booths.

"No way," he told Berg. "I don't *shlep*. Have Kassap deliver it. I'm not a goddamn taxi service. I'm not his supermarket delivery boy."

Berg shrugged. "Gerry might not like it."

"I don't much give a shit what Gerry likes. You just tell him if he doesn't want to spend the rest of his life picking rags to get the stock to my house tomorrow."

The next day, Kassap delivered about $10 million worth of numbered stock to Levy's home. Levy was watching for him, so he went out to meet him when he drove up. In the car, Levy noticed, was a gun—"not a gun, a cannon. Some people carry thirty-eights for personal protection. That's not a bad gun. Most cops carry them. Well, Kassap had a forty-five. Next to that, a thirty-eight looks like a dime-store toy. You get hit with a slug from a forty-five, and they can put a freeway through the hole."

Levy didn't know if Kassap had always carried the gun, or if he was carrying it because he was afraid of him.

"I didn't ask him either," he admits.

But Levy did ask Kassap if he could get more stock later, after they disposed of what he had then.

"Sure, no problem. I can just go back up north next time Brinks brings a shipment there."

Levy, still unaware that the Brinks/northern California story was a fabrication, said he was glad to hear that.

"Not that I ever thought we'd need more. I mean if I just got rid of the ten million I had, I could retire. And we figured there was another thirty million, maybe forty million dollars in numbered stock certificates that we could take care of right away. That would still leave us about seven hundred and fifty million dollars' worth of merchandise to play with."

Levy hid the first $10 million worth of stock in his house—buried in dirt, behind the furnace, in his unfinished basement—and then sat back to wait for Rod to call Jack Lane or Cabot Jones from Montreal ("or New York or the

Bahamas or wherever"). When Rod finally called Lane, it was to say he couldn't come to Los Angeles after all. He had too many other commitments to fly across the country on what he called "a maybe/maybe not deal." But he left a telephone number with Lane "in case one of you guys want to talk some more about this."

Lane sent Ryan to Levy's house with the message, and Levy—increasingly anxious to turn the stock into spendable cash so he could pay a few bills, feed his wife and baby and start eating decently again himself—walked down to the tennis club to call Rod.

Levy was still reluctant to be too specific about the deal on the phone. He didn't know who might be listening in on another extension at the club, and he always figured any phone he used might be tapped.

"Besides," he says, "I didn't know Rod. He was Jones' friend, not mine. I didn't want to spill my guts to him, and have him try to take over the whole deal."

Levy did tell Rod enough to whet his appetite, though. He mentioned that the deal involved stock—"a lot of stock, nine figures' worth"—and that it wasn't stolen or counterfeit. Rod was interested, but he still didn't want to fly to Los Angeles, so Levy volunteered to fly to New York. Rod liked that idea.

"Rod said if I had what I said I had, he could probably unload it for me, and pay me twenty-five cents on the dollar," Levy says. "I couldn't wait to get to New York. I'd been thinking ten cents, and he was offering twenty-five cents. I'd made two hundred and fifty percent profit already! I wouldn't even tell my partners. Fifteen cents off the top for me—zoop! in my pocket—then split the ten cents with them. On just the ten million dollars I had at home, that would mean almost three hundred fifty thousand bucks each for Steve and Kassap. They sure wouldn't bitch about that. They never even heard of such money. I could use my three hundred fifty thousand dollars to give

Jack Lane and his friends a commission, and I'd have my fifteen cents off the top—a cool one-and-a-half-million bucks —all to myself. And this was just the beginning. There was jillions more where that came from!"

Levy and Rod agreed to meet the following Sunday afternoon in the Delmonico Hotel on Park Avenue in midtown Manhattan.

Levy got his $2.98 briefcase out, and assembled a few samples of the stock certificates—"like a traveling salesman I was, going on the road with my sample case. Avon calling." Then he finagled a couple of relatives into loaning him $400 so he could buy a round-trip plane ticket to New York. He left Los Angeles late Saturday night on a TWA flight that "made so many stops and connections, I thought it was a 1948 milk run, not a 1971 transcontinental jet flight." But he had deliberately booked just such a flight, carefully avoiding a non-stop through flight. He even insisted on landing at LaGuardia Airport, usually used only for short-range flights, rather than John F. Kennedy Airport, where most cross-country flights come in.

Why?

"Because I was a sophisticated swindler. If anyone's following me or trying to pin something on me later, I got a great alibi. No big-time criminal takes a milk run that stops in Cincinnati and St. Louis and all those other garden spots of North America, right? He'd take a non-stop straight to Kennedy—zip, zop, zoop. Not me. I'm too smart for that. Besides, I'm not taking any chances. I don't even carry my briefcase on the plane with me. I check it through with the rest of the luggage on the flight—with no name tag or anything. That way, if someone is following me—or waiting for me in New York—I got nothing incriminating on me, and I can walk away clean and leave the briefcase. What do I care about losing a few samples? I got millions more where that came from. Zillions." He pauses. "Of course, no one's following me, and no one's waiting for me. No one even gives a shit who I am." He pauses again. "I got one problem, though: I got terrible cramps, and I can't go to the toilet on an airplane. It's a thing with me. Not even my psychiatrist could figure it out completely. Something to do with insecurity and thinking of my home as a womb and being afraid when I'm away from it. 'Cause it's not just airplanes. I can't go to the toilet in restaurants either —no place except wherever is home then, whether it's an actual house or an apartment or a hotel room. But no airplanes or restaurants or ball games or anything like that.

"I remember one time a couple of years earlier, my wife and I were at the opening of *Fiddler on the Roof* at the Music Center in Los Angeles and I had a tux on and I felt like I had to go to the bathroom something awful. I had excruciating cramps. But I knew if I got up in the middle of the show to go to the bathroom, I'd disturb everyone around me, and when I got to the toilet, I wouldn't be able to go anyway. Well, finally, I just couldn't stand it any more. It was agony. I was dying. I jumped up, stepped on both my wife's feet, tromped on three other people and went racing, tails flying, into the men's room. My clothes felt like they were choking me, and the minute I got into a stall, I took them off, every stitch. And, sure enough, I couldn't go. I broke into a cold sweat. My cramps got worse and worse. I thought, 'Oh, my God, I'm going to pass out cold, stark naked, on the floor of the Music Center toilet, and they're going to send those ushers in after me—the ones with the funny uniforms—and they're going to carry me out just as the show breaks, and the first person we're going to pass is my wife.'"

The anguish wasn't quite that exquisite on the long flight to New York "but it was close," Levy says. "I usually flirt like crazy with the stewardesses. This time, I just held my gut and groaned a lot."

The plane landed at LaGuardia about 7 A.M.—in freezing cold and a snowstorm—and Levy, with his coat collar pulled up around his ears, peering around as if he were surrounded by FBI agents, went to claim his briefcase in the baggage area.

When he stepped outside, the cold wind almost cut him in half.

"It had been gorgeous when we left L.A., and I land in weather that feels like a hundred below, and I'm not dressed for it. I got a turtleneck sweater and a medium-weight leather coat on, with no lining, and I'm freezing my ass off. I couldn't afford a cab, so I took a bus into the city. I got there about eight o'clock, and I'm not supposed to see Rod till noon. You ever try to kill four hours in New York on a Sunday morning—in a snowstorm? Nothing's open. No shops, no restaurants, nothing. I wanted to go to a movie, but I was afraid some fag'd grope me at that time of day. I started to go to the park, but I just knew I'd get mugged. So I walked from the East Side Terminal, on Thirty-Seventh Street and First Avenue, up into the Eighties on Park Avenue and then back down Lexington and up Madison. I walked and walked and walked. I didn't see a soul, and I damn near froze to death. I felt like I was in one of those science-fiction movies where the whole world has been destroyed and I was the only survivor.

"Finally, I got so cold, I walked into a hotel and sat down in the lobby. Great idea, right? Why didn't I think of this sooner, I'm asking myself. Well, ten minutes after I sit down, the bell captains and desk clerks start looking at me like I'm a leper. A *schlub* like me obviously isn't registered there. I start to get a complex, and I decide I'll call Rod now, even if it is only eleven o'clock."

Levy expected Rod to be as excited as he was about the deal, but Rod barely seemed to remember his name. And he was busy just then anyway—"in a meeting." Levy, he said, should come to his hotel at noon, as previously arranged.

Levy started walking again. Rod, he decided, had probably acted as he had on the telephone because he was with other people, and didn't want to risk their learning anything about his pending transactions with Levy. Smart man, Levy figured; about time someone showed a little brains and discretion.

Curiously, the closer it got to noon that Sunday in New York, the warmer Levy began to feel.

"The weather was still cold," he says, "but I was already counting my money. I could almost feel my money keeping me warm. From freezing fucking New York, my mind has me in Miami Beach, by the pool, counting my money."

When he walked into the Delmonico, Levy called Rod's room, assuming he would be invited up. Instead, Rod said he'd be right down.

"I didn't much like that—until I saw him. He was in his early fifties, very polished and distinguished looking. I felt better already. Then he took me into a restaurant in the hotel. It was actually closed—no waiters or customers or anything—but the door was open. We sit down, and he points to my briefcase and says, 'Okay, show me what you got.' He didn't ask, 'How was your trip?' or 'How you feeling?' Not even 'Good morning.' Just, 'Okay, show me what you got.'"

Levy was as taken aback by Rod's abruptness as he was by the suggestion that he display his merchandise in a public restaurant—even one that was closed and empty. He looked around, satisfied himself that they were still alone and opened the briefcase.

"When I handed him the stock, he handled it the way I should have been handling it from the beginning. He picked it up with his fingernails, and held it on the very edge. I'd been handling it like a sack of groceries. My fingerprints were all over the stuff."

Rod told Levy the certificates looked authentic.

"Where'd you get them?" he asked.

Levy told him the whole story. When he was through, Rod—who had been carefully examining the stock throughout his explanation—said, "Well, these are very rough, indeed. I can't take them like this. You'll have to prepare them."

Levy was dumbfounded: "Rough? Prepare? What is this —a delicatessen? A brisket he wants I should prepare? I thought you said they were authentic."

Patiently, Rod begins to explain.

"There are a lot of things that are normally done to stock certificates after they're printed but before they're actually issued. First, these have to be made out in a street name. You—"

Levy interrupted. "Street name? What do you mean—Broadway? Park Avenue?"

Rod, uncertain if Levy was really that stupid—or just that poor a jokester—resumed his explanation:

"No, they have to be filled out in someone's name, whoever the owner is supposed to be." He waved aside Levy's second interruption. "You can just pick a name out of the telephone book, if you want." Then he began pointing to various spots on the certificates. "You'll also need a date stamp here and a transfer agent's signature here and a recorder's signature here and a signature guarantee stamp here. The last one's the most important. If you make these out in a street name—say to John Smith—you'll have to sign them off 'John Smith' on the back to make them negotiable. You can't do that unless someone in a bank or a brokerage house guarantees that that's really John Smith's signature."

By this time, Levy's head was swimming. What had started out as a lark was growing in complexity far beyond his limited knowledge. But he didn't want Rod to think he was completely ignorant. So he just kept saying, "No problem. Sure, we can handle that." As they were getting ready to leave, Levy asked, "After I take care of all that stuff, how much can you use?"

"About two hundred fifty thousand dollars."

"That's all? I figured a big operator like you could dump a few million bucks' worth."

"Let's see how the first two hundred fifty thousand goes, okay? If we don't have any problems with that, I'm sure we'll be able to do business again."

Levy said he assumed the twenty-five-cents-on-the-dollar offer was still good.

"No," Rod told him, "that was for fully prepared stock. With you doing the preparation, I'm taking more risk."

Levy started to object, but Rod cut him off.

"Look, you can figure on anywhere between ten cents and twenty cents on the dollar. But let's see what your handiwork looks like before we firm up any specific figure, okay?"

Levy agreed, and Rod told him to call when the stock was ready.

"He gave me phone numbers in Montreal and New York and the Bahamas, and I'm thinking, 'How the hell am I going to carry around enough quarters to call all over the world? My pants will be so heavy, I'll be walking around like a little kid with crap in his diapers.'"

But Levy didn't tell Rod he couldn't even afford a telephone.

"I'll call you as soon as I'm ready to move," he said.

The two men shook hands and bantered briefly about the weather before Rod excused himself to return to his room.

Levy waited for him to disappear inside the elevator. He didn't want Rod to see that he couldn't afford a cab ride to the airport either.

As soon as the hotel elevator began its ascent, with Rod inside, Levy left the Delmonico and walked back to the East Side Terminal. There he bought a Hershey bar—his only "meal" of the day—and took a bus to the airport. The flight home was discouraging. He had expected to return to Los Angeles with a commitment that would make him rich; instead, he had a tentative offer that probably wouldn't net him more than $25,000 or so. Still, he had to admit, that wasn't bad money for a quick trip to New York. And he was learning something every day—knowledge he could put to good use in disposing of the rest of the stock. By the time he landed in Los Angeles, he had talked himself out of the temporary depression. But he had also begun to feel the first symptoms of a cold brought about by his exposure to the frigid elements in New York. Within a few days, the cold would give way to a mild case of pneumonia. ("I go to New York for *gelt*," he grumbled to his wife, "and I come back with germs.")

Levy didn't spend much time feeling sorry for himself, though. He had more important things to do—and he began by contacting a couple of his friends on the periphery of the Mafia. Levy's father had known several mafiosos in Chicago—had been their dentist, in fact—and he'd been fascinated with their life-style. When Alan grew up, he found them equally irresistible. When he'd owned his dress stores in Los Angeles in the 1960's, he'd mingled with a few friends of mobster Mickey Cohen, and he'd spent most of his evenings at P.J.'s, a popular nightclub frequented by many of the gamblers, shylocks and other shady characters who populate the big city by night. Between those contacts and his gambling and bookmaking, he came to know a number of underworld figures, and now he thought they might be able to tell him how to prepare the stock for Rod; they might even help him unload the stock themselves. Fortunately, Levy suffered a rare attack of good judgment when he talked to his friends. He prudently withheld most of the details, and was careful not to tell them just how much money could be involved. They said they thought their "associates" might be interested, but by the time they got back to Levy, it was clear that their "associates" would want an even bigger piece of the action than Rod wanted.

Levy, if he were lucky, might be left with a few crumbs. He said he'd go elsewhere.

Elsewhere turned out to be one brokerage house after another. Posing as a potential client, he asked questions that prompted brokers to show him a wide variety of stock certificates. He studied all of them. Within a week, he learned most of what he needed to know. Once he knew where and how to date-stamp his certificates, he bought several 1970 and 1971 date stamps from a stationery store in Beverly Hills. Once he knew where and how to fill out the street name, he selected several names at random from the Los Angeles telephone directory. Once he knew where the signatures of the recorder and transfer agent went—and what they looked like—he selected two such names at random from the other certificates the brokers were showing him. The transfer agent was by far the most important of the two. His signature would be taken as evidence that the stock had, indeed, been issued. As long as the signature looked authentic, the banker making a loan on Levy's stock would be highly unlikely to call the transfer agent to verify issuance of the stock. Or so Levy had been told. Thus, it was imperative that Levy select a transfer agent's name that was either so common or so genuine no one would give it a second thought. By an incredible stroke of blind luck—selecting at random from the hundreds of stock certificates he was shown—Levy decided to use the name J. J. O'Brien as the transfer agent on his first batch of stock— the International Chemical and Nuclear Corp. stock. J. J. O'Brien, it turned out, was the transfer agent who worked for Chase Manhattan Bank of New York, and actually signed the International Chemical and Nuclear Corp. stock certificates. The name Levy signed would be a forgery, but at least it would be a forgery of the right name.

That left Levy with one final problem in the preparation of the stock—the signature guarantee stamp. The only solution to the problem, he decided, was to steal one. But

Levy is a big schemer, not a petty thief. After several half-hearted attempts to steal a stamp from various brokers, he gave up and went looking for a professional burglar.

"I'd thought it would be easy to steal one myself," he says. "I figured I could just distract a broker's attention for a minute and—zoop!—off his desk and into my pocket. But someone was always watching me. At least, that's how I felt by then. So I said fuck it, and I got a hold of a friend of mine who happened to be a very good burglar."

The friend told Levy he'd do the job for $1,000. A few days later, the friend called back to say he'd found an easier way to get the signature guarantee stamp—a banker he knew would steal one for him. That way, he said, there would be no illegal break-in. Levy said that would be fine, but how much did the banker want?

"Five hundred dollars."

"Okay."

A week went by. Two weeks went by. Still no signature guarantee stamp. Levy couldn't find his burglar, and he didn't know who the burglar's banker was. More out of frustration and boredom than anything else, he returned to one of the Beverly Hills brokerage houses he'd visited earlier. During a conversation with one of the brokers he'd gotten to know rather well, he casually asked what a signature guarantee stamp looked like. The broker showed him.

"But what does the stamp really say?" Levy asked.

The broker took a small, blank piece of paper out of his desk and stamped it. Levy looked at it, then resumed the conversation. Twenty minutes later, when he got up to leave, he casually picked up the piece of paper and stuffed it in his pocket. Later that same day, he took the piece of paper to a little shop that makes rubber stamps, and asked them to make him one "just like this."

Two days later, he picked the stamp up. It cost him $9—"plus tax."

"And they never even asked if I was from the brokerage house or had the authorization to get the stamp made or anything. Just 'That'll be nine dollars, please.'"

With his sophisticated swindler's tool-kit now complete, Levy was ready to begin. He borrowed an electric typewriter from Steve Berg, installed himself in his sister-in-law's back bedroom—without giving her the slightest hint of what he was up to—and went quickly to work. But he had forgotten one item.

"As soon as I started signing and stamping and all, I remembered how Rod had been so careful handling the stock. I asked one of my shady friends how I could keep my fingerprints off, and he said I should buy a pair of thin rubber surgical gloves. Brilliant idea! They lasted about thirty minutes. The way I sweat, they were filled up with water before I had three certificates finished. It was a riot. Here I am trying to get the right dates and signatures on, very neatly, no mistakes, and I'm dripping water on the certificates like I'm working in a steambath. I didn't even have to take the gloves off. They floated off."

No sooner had Levy resolved that problem than he encountered another—some of the certificates had a silver-leaf overlay where one of the signatures was supposed to go. Levy's ballpoint pen wouldn't write over the silver. He tried another kind of pen. No luck. He went to a stationery store and bought a dozen different pens. Still no luck. Finally, he bought a fiber-tip pen—a Flair. That did the trick, and Levy went back to work.

"It was an incredible scene," he says. "I was sitting in this bedroom surrounded by all this stock, and I've got two date stamps, a typewriter, my handy-dandy signature guarantee stamp and three different kinds of pens. I type in the 'street names,' use the stamps, sign here, sign there and —zip, zop, zoop—the certificate is done. But I gotta make things look legitimate. I can't have one guy owning all the stock. And I can't have all the transactions with the same date. Or all the signatures looking alike. So I'm alternating names and staggering the dates and I'm signing right-handed and lefthanded and two-handed and sideways and upside down and with one eye closed and the other eye closed and both eyes closed, and I've got certificates scattered all over the room, and half the time I can't find the right pen or the right stamp, and I'm not exactly the world's greatest typist, so I have to go slow to avoid mistakes . . ."

It took Levy several days to finish preparing the stock. Then he walked over to the tennis club and called Rod in Montreal. He wasn't there. Levy tried New York. Not there. The Bahamas. Not there. He left messages everywhere for Rod to call him through Jack Lane, and by then, he was out of change. He bummed a dime from the club tennis pro and called Lane. Lane said he didn't have any other numbers for Rod, but he would tell everyone in his office to be on the alert for a call from him. Three days later, Rod called Lane and left a number where he could be reached.

Lane drove to Levy's house with the number, and Levy sprinted to the tennis club to call.

"I wanted to bitch at him for taking so long, but I couldn't take the chance that he might get pissed and call the whole thing off," he says. "I had to be nice."

Levy and Rod arranged to meet at a brokerage house in Vancouver, where Rod had to go on another business deal. But he told Levy to bring just $100,000 worth of stock along. When Levy started to protest that he had asked for $250,000, Rod cut him off with, "I'll pay you twenty cents on the dollar." Levy did some quick mental calculations: "That's twenty thousand dollars—ten thousand off the top for me since my partners still think I'm only getting ten cents on the dollar. Ten thousand. Not exactly a million dollars, but it's a start."

Borrowing from his relatives again, Levy buys a round-trip ticket to Vancouver. But he has a vague, hazy recollection of some law prohibiting American citizens from carrying large amounts of cash or negotiable securities out of the country. That eliminates the briefcase. He can't make like a traveling salesman this time; what if the Customs officers search his luggage? He decides he'll have to carry the stock on his body. But $100,000 worth of stock certificates can be pretty bulky. How will he conceal them? He tosses and turns the better part of a night before he hits on an idea. Early the next morning, he goes to the neighborhood grocery store and buys several boxes of Baggies—small plastic bags generally used for sandwiches in children's lunches. He carefully folds the certificates and puts them in the Baggies. Then he tapes the Baggies to his chest and back with Ace bandages, and dons a heavy, wool turtleneck sweater.

"The sweater was bulky-knit, so nothing looked suspicious," he says. "Besides, I was going to Vancouver in February. It's cold as a son-of-a-bitch up there then. I figured the guys in Customs would expect people to be all bundled up."

That day, Levy left Los Angeles for Vancouver, feeling very pleased with himself. The feeling lasted roughly ten minutes—about as long as it took for the Western Airlines jet to get off the ground. That's when Levy discovered that the air conditioning vents on the plane weren't working.

"I was sitting there with this heavy sweater on, sweating like a pig, and they got no goddamn air conditioning. On top of everything, the sweater is scratchy. So are the Baggies. And the tape itches like crazy. And it's pulling the hair on my chest. The people sitting near me must have thought I'd gone bananas. I was jerking and fidgeting and sweating and *shvitzing* and scratching, and the more I scratched, the worse it got. I started to worry about how suspicious I looked, and that only made me sweat more. And itch more. And scratch more. And sweat more. The flight was two and a half hours, and by the time we landed in Vancouver, even my sweat was sweating."

As soon as he saw the Customs officers, he felt even worse.

"Oh my God," he thought, "they're going to know I've got the stuff. They'll throw me in a room and undress me and find it and I'll spend the rest of my life in a Canadian prison."

Levy had lived in Canada—in Peterborough, Ontario—with his mother and stepfather from the time he was eleven until the time he was eighteen, and his memories of the country were not especially warm. He didn't want to spend time in a hotel there, no less a prison.

Struggling for his self-control, Levy wisely decided to stand near the middle of the line going through Customs —both to give himself a chance to retain his composure and, he hoped, to more easily fade into the crowd. All his worries were for naught. The Customs agent barely glanced at him and said, "You, through" and he was in Canada. But he practically knocked a guard over in his mad dash for the men's room. Once safely inside, he pawed in his pants pocket for a dime, locked himself in a pay toilet, tore the sweater off and began ripping the tape off—"taking about three layers of skin along with it."

He stuffed the stock in the pockets of his raincoat—"I came prepared this time, thank God; it was pouring"—and took a cab to Rod's brokerage house.

Canadian brokerage houses are, in many ways, more like Japanese houses than American houses. Penny mining stocks are traded frantically in an atmosphere of barely controlled frenzy, amid the clatter of ticker tapes and shouts of buy and sell orders. Into this chaos strode Alan Levy.

"Rod was busy just then. He put me in a private office, and said he'd see me as soon as he could. About an hour later, he walked in and I showed him the stock. He was very pleased. He said everything looked very good, and we'd go straight to his bank.

"When we got to the bank, I knew I was home free. The vice president came over right away and gave Rod the red-carpet treatment. He was obviously a very good customer. Rod introduced me, and explained what we wanted and the vice president just said, 'Fine, fine. I'm sure we can accommodate you, gentlemen.' He even looked the stock up in *Standard and Poor*, and told us what a good, sound stock it was. I was ecstatic. Even when he said it was so late in the day we'd have to come back in the morning to pick up our money, I kept smiling. Hell, what's a night in Vancouver when you're going to get ten thousand dollars for breakfast? We finished the paperwork, and Rod started to pick up the stock and told the vice president he'd bring it back and turn it over when we picked up the money.

"Oh, no, no," the vice president said. "Our bank has a policy of checking all stock left for collateral. We'll have to call the transfer agent in New York first thing tomorrow. That's why we can't consummate the loan right now. Purely routine, of course."

Of course.

Rod surrenders the stock and says, "Fine. We'll—"

Levy, suddenly sweating again, nudges him discreetly. Rod ignores him and continues speaking—"We'll be glad to leave it with you."

By now Levy's nudge is more like a shove. Still Rod continues blithely on. Levy whispers desperately in his ear, "We can't leave this. There was no transfer agent for this stock, remember? *I'm* J. J. O'Brien." Rod keeps talking. Levy on the verge of apoplexy, snatches the stock from the vice president's desk—"It's mine!"—and Rod smoothly tells the vice president he and Levy "have just a point or two to discuss first." Even as he's saying those words, Levy is bolting for the door—leaving a shocked and bewildered bank staff in his wake, certain the Royal Canadian Mounted Police are already after him.

Outside, Levy explodes at Rod:

"I thought you were a big-brain wheeler-dealer. What the hell did you think was going to happen if we left that stock?"

Rod says he didn't understand. "I thought, I mean, that is, I—"

Levy isn't interested in any further discussion. He turns his back on Rod, leaving him in mid-sentence, hails a cab and rides in bitter, furious silence to the airport.

"I was so pissed, I didn't give a good goddamn if I got caught going through Customs or not. I carried the stock stuffed in my raincoat pockets. No one stopped me, but if they had, I would've told them I'd found the stuff in a pay toilet. That's where it belonged, all that crap!"

The minute Levy got back to Los Angeles, he called Berg and told him to have Kassap come pick up the stock —all of it.

"I'd spent over five hundred dollars to go to New York and Vancouver. I'd blown almost a month with the *farkokte* date stamps and Flair pens and signature guarantee stamps and Ace bandages and Baggies and phone calls and waiting and meetings. I'd been in a rainstorm and a snowstorm. I'd caught pneumonia. I'd seen a potential million-dollar deal with Rod drop to two hundred fifty thousand, then a hundred thousand. My big eight-hundred-million-dollar score went all the way down to ten thousand dollars—the fastest drop of any stock in the history of the world—and then I didn't even get the ten thousand dollars. Shit, I didn't even get a chance to cheat my partners. I got *bubkes*, and they got *bubkes*. What the fuck kind of scam was that? I wanted out—now!"

The next day, Kassap came to Levy's house to pick up the stock.

"I told Kassap I was retiring. My career as a sophisticated international stock-swindler was over, through, *fini*. I was going back to earning money the easy way—stealing atomic secrets and selling them to the king of Lithuania."

Chapter 3

L evy's "retirement" was short-lived.

It took him about three weeks to recover, emotionally and physically, from the exhaustion, the pneumonia and the disappointment, and then he was at loose ends again —still broke and still bored. With nothing better to do, he stopped by Jack Lane's office one afternoon. While he and Levy were talking, two men walked in—a tall, goateed black man and his white chauffeur.

The black man was Tom Wilson, a movie producer who had been introduced to Lane by Fred Ryan earlier in the year. Wilson was trying to finance a movie he wanted to make in Europe. Lane, he thought, might be able to help him.

"What he wanted," Levy recalls, "was a good financial statement—a statement heavy enough to take to Dun and Bradstreet and get a good credit rating, so he could walk into any bank in Europe and get financing for his picture. About all he had on his financial statement right then, he said, was four hundred thousand dollars. That sounded pretty good to me, so I chimed into the conversation."

"What's the four hundred thousand dollars in?" Levy asked.

"My scripts," Wilson replied.

"Your who?"

"My scripts."

Levy was aghast. "Banks don't lend money on scripts any more. You couldn't get a quarter—a dime. You need tangible assets—stocks, bonds, real estate, oil, like that."

Wilson looked to Lane as if to say, "Who the hell's this idiot, and what's he doing here?" But when Lane nodded in confirmation of what Levy had said, Wilson turned to Levy and said, "What can I do, then?"

Levy, struggling to keep the smugness out of his voice, just said quietly, "Well, let's go get a cup of coffee next door. I think I may have your problem solved."

Over coffee, Levy told Wilson he had a friend who might be willing to put $1 million worth of stock temporarily in Wilson's name—or, rather, in the name of his production company. That ploy, Levy decided, was even better than using the stock as direct loan collateral. With Wilson, the stock would just be listed as an asset of the production company, verified by Dun and Bradstreet, and then Wilson would actually be borrowing money on his financial statement, not on the stock itself. But Levy couldn't take the risk that Wilson might decide to sell the stock while it was in his name, so—without telling him the entire story—he implied that the stock was of sufficiently shady origin that trying to sell it would be "like fitting yourself for a pair of bracelets."

"Our motto," Levy said, "is 'Flash but don't cash.' Remember: you can take the stock to Dun and Bradstreet and show it around all you want. But don't try to cash it. You cash the stock, and you go on a long vacation before you even got a chance to go home for your toothbrush." Wilson said he understood. "I hope you do," Levy told him, "because if you cash the stock, I never saw you before in my life."

Levy asked Wilson a few questions about the movie—

who wrote it, who's in the cast, what's the story line, who's the director—and he liked the answers.

"But why bother actually making the movie?" he asked Wilson. "How much you figure it'll cost?"

Wilson said he planned to borrow $600,000.

"Six hundred thousand?" Levy yelped. "Let's just borrow it and stick it in our pockets and run."

Wilson wouldn't hear of it. He was a producer, he said, and producers produce movies.

"Okay," Levy countered. "Let's make a movie for a hundred and fifty thousand dollars and stick four hundred and fifty thousand in our pocket and run."

Again, Wilson refused. Levy capitulated:

"Okay, here's the deal—I'll have a contract drawn up that gives me twenty-five thousand dollars up front, the minute you get the picture financed. I also get a guaranteed five percent of the gross and a job as assistant costume designer on the movie."

Wilson started to object that he couldn't have a stock manipulator "cluttering up my set as an assistant costume designer."

Levy haughtily informed him that he'd spent "most of my life in the ready-to-wear business, and I figure you're getting an expert at bargain basement prices."

For once, Levy wasn't bullshitting. He actually had spent more than fifteen years in the ready-to-wear business and had, in fact, been one of the first boutique-owners in Los Angeles to import French fashions. He'd gotten his start in the fashion industry in Chicago in the early 1950's, right after he finagled a medical discharge from the army because of his asthma attacks. He'd worked first as a janitor in his uncle's dress factory, then worked his way up to shipping clerk and, finally, salesman. He'd pocketed some money that should've gone into the cash register, so his uncle sent him out on the road. But he started writing bad checks to cover his gambling losses—and cashing the checks with his uncle's customers. His uncle fired him. Levy didn't tell Tom Wilson much about that experience, but he did remind him that he had owned two of the most successful boutiques in Beverly Hills—Alan Lewis and The Haberdashery—and that seemed to impress Wilson.

Wilson agreed to the job and the $25,000, but he said he couldn't surrender 5 percent of the gross. The two men sparred briefly, and finally settled on 2 1/2 percent.

Levy was very pleased with himself. The $25,000 was more than he had been expecting to get off the top with Rod in Vancouver, and if the movie was any good at all, his cut of the gross should at least double that. Black movies were big now, he figured, and Wilson's two stars were big box-office draws. Besides, the job as assistant costume designer would provide him with a legitimate cover for his share of the deal and give him a free trip to Europe and something to do with his time—as well as an opportunity to maybe learn an exciting new business. Who knows, he might like being in the movies. Or, more likely, he might meet a few more people who could use some of his stock.

"The best thing of all about the deal," Levy remembers thinking, "was that Wilson actually planned to make the movie and pay his loan back and return my stock to me. I was going to make good money for no risk at all really, and I'd still get my stock back to start all over or burn the evidence or whatever."

Levy and Wilson shook hands, and agreed to meet again soon. In the meantime, Levy would prepare the stock in the street name of Tom Wilson Productions Inc. That evening, Levy called Steve Berg and told him to have Kassap bring "a few million bucks' worth of stock back to my place. Make sure you include the stuff I prepared for Rod. I got us a live one." Levy figured it would take $1 million worth of stock for Wilson to make a $600,000 loan, and he wanted to have another $4 or $5 million ready just in case he needed it.

When Kassap delivered the stock, Levy once again assembled his tool kit of pens and stamps, picked up Berg's electric typewriter and returned to his sister-in-law's house for another round of stock preparation.

"By this time, I was an expert," he says. "I didn't sweat quite so much, and I had a pretty good idea what I was doing."

Once the stock was properly prepared—and returned to its hiding place in Levy's half-finished basement—Levy met with Wilson and his board of directors at Universal Studios.

"I went out there on a Saturday afternoon, all puffed up with how rich and famous I was going to be. A meeting at Universal Studios, with my very own producer, and my name in credits on the screen and twenty-five thousand dollars and two-and-a-half percent and—forget it; just call me Mr. DeMille."

But when Levy arrived at Universal, he found that Wilson's office wasn't on the studio lot proper; it was a small office in a building across the street and down the block, where Universal rented space.

Levy began having second thoughts, and when he met with Wilson's board of directors, he suggested having the stock made out in a fictitious street name, rather than in the name of Tom Wilson Productions. Then he would sign off the street name, just as he had done with the stock he took to Vancouver, and it would look like that fictional person had sold (or given or loaned) the stock to Tom Wilson. It could still be listed as an asset on Wilson's financial statement, but Wilson couldn't sell it. The board of directors wouldn't buy that, though. They—and Wilson—insisted on the original agreement; the stock must be listed in the production company's name, or there would be no deal.

To impress Levy with his contacts and his muscle, Wilson called London in the course of the meeting, and spoke briefly with Mario Denard, a man he described as "part of the Mafia from Cleveland." Levy, having had more than his share of Mafia contacts, wasn't particularly impressed: "When I met Denard, I found out I was right. He couldn't rob the blind man on the corner, this guy."

But on the phone that day, Wilson and Denard talked about all manner of underworld connections and people they knew in high finance and a big insurance company in Europe they could borrow the money from. When they were through, they had agreed it would be just as easy to borrow $750,000 as $600,000. That, of course, was fine with Levy and—despite his misgivings—he gave Wilson the stock.

"The easy thing for us to do then would have been to just hire an accountant to prepare a financial statement, and take the statement to Dun and Bradstreet, right? Well, when a crook's mind is working, he never thinks of the easy, direct approach. I decided we shouldn't go to Dun and Bradstreet with the statement up front, after all. They might get suspicious." He shakes his head. "Why should they get suspicious? People come in with financial statements all the time. But, all of a sudden, I think they're going to know by the way our shoes are shined that we're big swindlers. So I tell Wilson I know a guy who knows a guy who knows a guy who's friends with a guy who's an investigator for Dun and Bradstreet.

"Credit companies like that have their credit records on microfilm," I tell them, "and this investigator can microfilm our statement privately and just splice it into the Dun and Bradstreet records. No muss, no fuss. And he'll do it for a G-note, a grand, one thousand *zables*."

But Wilson said he'd rather use "one of our people"— meaning a black—if they were going to do the job surreptitiously. A couple of days later, Wilson, his chauffeur and Levy drove to a small office on Hollywood Boulevard, where Wilson introduced Levy to a black "preacher" he said specialized in phony drivers' licenses and Social Security cards.

"He graduated from Gezundheit Biblical College in East

Elephant's Breath, Louisiana, or some such place, so right away, I know he's a winner," Levy says. "How a preacher comes to phony drivers' licenses I still can't figure out. And what drivers' licenses have to do with financial statements . . . well, this whole thing's getting so confused, you need a program to tell the players."

But the preacher says he can do the job for $250.

"See," Wilson says. "We go to our people, and already we save seven hundred and fifty dollars. Your guy wanted one thousand."

Levy winced. "Tom, I'll tell you, I think we just got took for two hundred and fifty dollars. Your people, my people, nobody's people. We got about as much chance of getting into Dun and Bradstreet with that *cockamamy* preacher as we have of going to an orgy with the Queen of England."

When two weeks went by with no word from the preacher, Wilson tacitly admitted Levy had probably been right, and they decided to go the direct route. Wilson's accountant would draft a financial statement that included the stock—all of it International Chemical and Nuclear Corp. stock—and one of Wilson's associates would file the statement with Dun and Bradstreet. Wilson, meanwhile, would fly to London, so he could apply for the loan as soon as the Dun and Bradstreet credit rating was circulated.

But Dun and Bradstreet wasn't about to accept some accountant's statement that Tom Wilson Productions Inc. was suddenly worth more than $1 million—not when Wilson himself, as Levy later learned, had a criminal record as a drug-pusher. They wanted to see the stock certificates themselves. That was fine, except for one thing—Wilson and the stock were already in London; he had assumed he would be more likely to need it there, when he actually consummated the loan, than in Los Angeles. Everyone panicked; if they couldn't show the stock to Dun and Bradstreet, Dun and Bradstreet might *really* think there was something fishy going on. When Dun and Bradstreet called Wilson's office, the office put them in touch with Wilson's vice president. The vice president went looking for Levy— who, of course, still didn't have a telephone at home.

"Everyone is running around, wringing their hands and screaming 'What are we going to do? What are we going to do?'" Levy says. "The whole deal is collapsing, and Tom Wilson is sitting on his ass in London, oblivious to everything."

Finally, Levy suggests what should have been obvious to all of them: "Call Tom in London, and tell him to take the stock to the Dun and Bradstreet office there. Let them examine the stock and Telex their confirmation to Dun and Bradstreet in L.A. Tell Tom to offer to pay for the Telex or any transatlantic phone calls or any other charges. We're supposed to be big businessmen, remember. We got a million-dollar statement. Let's act like it."

By this time, Levy was getting fed up with driving his little Fiat. He figured he could parlay the Tom Wilson financial statement and his position as assistant costume designer into a new car. He visited a leasing agent in Beverly Hills, and by the time he got through talking to him—"a little dipsy-do here, a zippety-do-dah there"—he had leased new cars for most of the board of directors—"three Cadillac Eldorados, a Lincoln and two Oldsmobile Cutlass convertibles."

Levy kept a beige Cadillac with saddle-brown interior for himself—"a nice, inconspicuous car, you know, something I could slip in and out of town in, unobtrusive-like. Slip in and out of town? Christ, I couldn't even slip in and out of my driveway. The fucking car was too goddamn big for my garage."

The new car didn't keep Levy happy very long, though. He couldn't buy groceries or clothes or pay off bookies with a car—not even a Cadillac Eldorado. When he had not heard from anyone in Wilson's office after two or three weeks, he started to get uneasy again. He called Wilson's vice president, and the two of them met on his boat.

"Don't worry," he told Levy. "Tom thinks he can get a loan from the Transcaribbean Bank and—"

Levy cut in. "The Transwhobian Bank? What kind of bank is that? Where the hell do they get seven hundred fifty thousand dollars to loan us? That's like having someone pay you with a check drawn on the First National Bank of Budapest."

Wilson's vice president insisted everything was okay, and said Wilson would be back "as soon as he gets through with a few preliminary arrangements for the film."

Levy snorted in disgust. "This whole thing is beginning to sound like an all-expense-paid European vacation for Tom Wilson. All I know is, he better show up fast. I want my money, and if I don't get it pretty soon, I got a friend who can eat your Tom Wilson and his Mario Denard for breakfast."

While he was waiting to hear from Wilson, Levy came home one day and found a note stuck under his front door. ("That's how all us sophisticated criminals operate, right?") The note was from Fred Ryan, the guy who had been running in and out of the office the night he first met with Jack Lane and Cabot Jones to discuss the stock. Ryan's note said he had to talk to Levy "right away."

Levy sprinted over to the tennis club—"as fast as my chubby little Jewish legs would carry me." He didn't know if Ryan had news of incipient disaster or a potential bonanza. It was, he soon learned, the latter. Ryan said he'd overheard just enough that night in Lane's office to get interested in the deal himself. He'd asked Lane a few questions, and filed the answers away for future use. The "future" had come sooner than he had expected. He knew a group of men—a psychologist and an attorney and a few businessmen—who might be interested in the stock. If

Levy would give him a few samples, he would see what they had in mind.

By this time, Levy wasn't going to give anyone any samples. ("Samples? What'd they think I was—a new soap company?") He'd made fruitless trips to New York and Vancouver, he'd had more meetings than Henry Kissinger, and now Tom Wilson was in London with $1 million worth of his stock. He told Ryan he'd deliver the samples himself. "Just tell me where and when."

Later that day, Ryan picked Levy up in his car.

"I took one look at it and thought, 'Oh, my God, here we go again.' It was a 1956 Mercury that barely made it out of my driveway, and Ryan—with his bloodshot eyes and pants that he must have been wearing for six years straight, without changing, looked even worse than the car. I was off and running with another zillion-dollar partner."

As the first steps of the new negotiations unfolded, Levy did, indeed, begin to feel a strangely discomfiting sense of *deja vu*. The way Ryan had described his friends, Levy expected them to be occupying wood-paneled, lushly carpeted offices in a beautiful new skyscraper. After all, their address was a Brentwood address, and Brentwood—sandwiched among Bel Air, Beverly Hills and Pacific Palisades—is one of Los Angeles' most fashionable suburbs. But Ryan took him to a small, second-story office in a nondescript building—"the only nondescript building in all of Brentwood," Levy says, "and that's where my partners gotta have an office. Naturally. Of course. What did I expect—a palace?"

The office, Levy says, looked like the lobby of a cheap motel—"nicer than Jack Lane's office on La Cienega, but not by much." A few minutes after Ryan introduced him to the five other men in the office, Levy began to feel as if he were actually back in Lane's office that very first night. In Lane's office, Ryan had been running in and out, causing a commotion. In the Brentwood office, as the men got

down to business, a woman kept banging on the front
door, screaming that one of the men inside was her boy
friend and she had to see him because he'd cheated her
out of her Cadillac. They said her boy friend wasn't there.
("He was hiding in an adjacent office," Levy says, shaking
his head incredulously.)

At the same time, three telephones in the office were
jangling incessantly, and yet another man was running in
and out, shouting, "I want my money. I want my money.
You owe me two hundred dollars."

Levy wanted to leave. "They couldn't pay him two hundred dollars; how were they going to deal in zillions with
me? We were all in a crazy house, and I was beginning to
feel like the senior inmate."

Finally, infuriated, Levy told one of the men, "Look, you
either put a stop to this three-ring circus, or me and my
stock are going home. When I want to deal with Ringling
Brothers, I'll call Ringling Brothers."

Quickly, the intruders were silenced, all the doors were
locked and—the din now diminished to just the ringing of
the telephones—Levy told the men about the stock. As he
spoke, two of the men—Gordon Iler and Ralph Ernsten
—began to take charge of the meeting. Iler was almost six
feet tall, heavy-set, with an honest moon-face that made
him look like a pillar of the community—"a deacon of the
church at least," Levy says. Ernsten was about two inches
taller and rail-thin, with his dark hair cut and greased in
a 1950s-style pompadour. Ernsten was no deacon, though;
Levy didn't know it then, but Ernsten had a long criminal
record, including convictions for forgery, larceny and mail
fraud, among other things.

Once Levy showed his samples to the men, Ernsten said
he thought he had two contacts who could prove invaluable
if Levy were interested in pursuing the matter. One of his
contacts was in the FBI. He would be able to tip them off
if anyone in law enforcement caught on to what they were

doing. Ernsten's other contact, he said, was a "Mr. Todd" —a big financier who had Swiss banking connections and was just then involved in the Penn Central Railroad bankruptcy proceedings.

In fact, Ernsten suggested, why didn't he call Mr. Todd right then. He was in La Jolla, near San Diego. Good idea, Levy said. It was about time he met someone who wanted to move immediately.

Ernsten made the call—a conversation that impressed Levy both for its discreet circumlocutions and for its smooth professionalism. "This guy," Levy says, "used all the right words and none of the wrong ones. He was a real pro. Just before he hung up, I heard him say, 'Fine then, you can consummate the transaction then on a sixty percent collateralized basis, and we'll have our money in five or six days. Very well. Thank you, Mr. Todd. We'll get back to you.'"

When Ernsten hung up, he turned to Levy and said, "Okay, he can handle five million dollars to start with. He'll place it in Swiss banks as collateral for a loan. He's going to play it conservatively. He could probably get a four-million-dollar loan for it, maybe more, but no sense in taking chances with a good thing. He'll just make a three-million loan. You get half to divide with your partners, and I'll take half to divide with Mr. Todd and my partners."

For a fleeting moment, it occurred to Levy that "Mr. Todd" was being extraordinarily generous. Cabot Jones' friend Rod had only offered to pay him twenty cents on the dollar. If Todd paid him $1.5 million—half the $3-million loan—for $5 million worth of stock, that was thirty cents on the dollar. But Levy felt he'd been screwed too many times himself to spend much time worrying about why someone else was being so generous to him. He did some quick mental calculations: He and Ryan had agreed to split whatever they got fifty-fifty. Ryan was sitting right there, so he couldn't very well screw him. That meant Ryan would get half the $1.5 million—$750,000—for himself, Cabot Jones and Jack Lane. Levy would pay Steve Berg and Gerald Kassap out of his $750,000.

"No way I'm going to split the seven hundred fifty thousand dollars in three equal shares," he thought as he sat there. "I'll tell them I got three hundred thousand. That's one hundred thousand for Steve, one hundred thousand for Kassap and five hundred fifty thousand for me. That's fair, right? I was running my ass off doing all the work and taking all the risks. Kassap was in his plant picking rags, and Steve was home reading the *Wall Street Journal*. Besides, when you get up into six and seven figures, you're not talking money any more, you're talking telephone numbers. Telephone numbers. Three hundred thousand, seven hundred fifty thousand, one million five hundred thousand, five million. With all those zeroes, it's like a telephone number—with an area code yet. It's playing Monopoly. 'You buy Boardwalk and I'll buy Park Place and you get three houses, and I get a hotel, and don't pass go and don't collect two hundred dollars.' What's it all mean anyway? Get your hands on any one of those six- or seven-figure deals and you're happy. A half-million-plus for me? Fine. Wonderful. A hundred thousand each for Steve and Kassap? Couldn't be better. I told Ernsten I liked his phone numbers. He could be in my phone book any day of the week."

Levy did have one question, though: How was Todd going to pay back the loan?

"Don't worry," Ernsten said, "he'll take care of it. We'll set up a dummy corporation, and list the stock as an asset of the corporation. We'll get someone to be the head of the corporation, and when the time comes, he'll take the fall. You don't have to concern yourself with that. He'll be paid well for what he does. You just get the five million dollars' worth of stock to us."

"When do you want it?"

"How about midnight tonight?"

"Okay. Where?"

"How about the Airport Marina Hotel?"

"Fine. Do you want all International Chemical and Nuclear stock, or should I give you some variety?"

"No, all of the one will be fine. We know that's a sound company."

Levy raised his eyebrows quizzically.

"I know it's solid, but that solid? I mean five million dollars' worth of stock would probably make us one of the biggest stockholders the company has in the whole world. Don't you think that might look just a little funny?"

Ernsten nodded. "Okay, mix it up. Put some other stuff in. But make it good stuff. No dogs."

"Who do you want it made out to?" Levy asked.

"No one. Just leave it blank for now. We'll take care of that."

Levy went back home, dug up some more stock from his basement hiding place, gathered up his stamps and pens and headed for his "office" in the back bedroom of his sister-in-law's house.

He didn't have too much work to do this time, since some of the stock had been prepared for the Vancouver trip; when he was through, he put the $5 million worth of certificates in a brown paper bag. ("I'd had it with the briefcase. I'd *shlepped* it to New York and Vancouver and Jack Lane's office and Tom Wilson's office and these guys' office, and I still didn't have a penny to show for my work. I figured maybe the paper sack would change my luck.")

Levy, daydreaming about what he was going to do with all his money, barely got the stock prepared in time. He had to race to the rendezvous point to make it by midnight. When he arrived at the hotel, Ernsten, Iler and a third man from that day's meeting were all waiting for him in a cocktail lounge. Ernsten had a girl with him, and he told Levy, "Her uncle's part of the Mafia in New Orleans."

Levy just chuckled to himself. "Everyone's in the Mafia," he says. "Guys brag about Mafia contacts in towns so small and remote, the local *capo* is probably a Filipino."

Levy turned the stock over to Ernsten and Iler, and asked them, "What's next?"

"It's going on a plane to New York," Iler told him. "Mr. Todd flew to New York already, and he'll pick it up there in the morning and be off to Switzerland."

Levy doesn't drink—and he was too tired for much small talk—so he didn't see any point in hanging around the cocktail lounge once he'd delivered the stock. "Just call me when you get the money," he said before he drove back home.

But Levy wasn't so sure he'd be hearing from Mr. Todd as quickly as Ernsten had promised. He went to see Fred Ryan, and told him they should contact Ernsten again.

"I can't wait for Mr. Todd to come wandering back from Switzerland, via New York, La Jolla and Southwest Cockalapedis," Levy told Ryan. "Ernsten once said we might be able to place small amounts of stock with a friendly banker somewhere for a quick loan; that's what I want—quick cash."

Ryan called Ernsten, and a meeting was arranged at a law office in Beverly Hills. The office was in a modern, ten-story bank building on one of the busiest corners in Beverly Hills. Most of the tenants of the building were attorneys, business managers, agents, consultants and other professional men. Levy liked the looks of it even before the attendant in the underground garage had parked his car. "This," he thought, "is more like it."

Levy and Ryan went upstairs, and Ryan introduced him to Martin Calaway, an attorney who leased the office. Bo Farmer was also there; he was the man who had been hiding from his girl friend during the earlier meeting with Iler and his friends in Brentwood. Iler was there, too. So were Cabot Jones and a couple of other men—including Ralph Ernsten, who assured Levy things were proceeding on schedule in Switzerland. "We should have our money any day now," he said.

After a bit of good-natured banter about how rich they would all soon be, Farmer explained that he had a company named Royal Viking in Phoenix, Arizona, and they wanted about $2.5 million worth of stock. As Farmer explained it, Royal Viking was going to place the stock in escrow with a broker, then show the record of that escrow to a bank and make a loan. The only possible hitch in that kind of deal, Farmer said, was the broker—"and this broker's in our pocket, so we got no problems at all."

Royal Viking only expected to need the loan for about ninety days, and they were willing to pay Farmer and his associates 10 percent of face value to let them hold the stock that long. That was $250,000—"off the top," Levy says. "We were going to get our cut from the money they borrowed, right up front."

Farmer said he would personally deliver the stock to Phoenix. That didn't exactly thrill Levy to death. He hardly knew Farmer. Nor was Ernsten especially enchanted by the suggestion. But they couldn't very well cut Farmer out; he had brought them the deal in the first place. After a brief discussion, they decided to send someone with him. Levy liked that idea until he saw the man Ernsten had in mind.

"Farmer was almost six foot tall, and the guy Ernsten wants to send, Bob Cox, looks like a midget—your kid brother who went to a *shvitz* and wasn't Sanforized and got shrunk. He had a crewcut, for Christ's sake, and those went out with God. That's who's gonna make sure we get our two hundred fifty thousand dollars?"

But Cox, though short, was well-built—squat and muscular—and Ernsten assured Levy he was "an ex-marine ... trained to kill."

While Ernsten and Levy were talking about who should accompany Farmer to Phoenix, Farmer was calling his contact there to confirm the transaction. Finally, everything was settled, and it was agreed that Levy would prepare $2.5 million worth of stock for Farmer and Ernsten's friend, Cox, to take to Phoenix.

But there was another item on the agenda of that particular meeting. A building contractor named Finn Konsmo, who lived in Orange County, southeast of Los Angeles, had been invited in because he said he had a friendly banker who might be willing to accept small amounts of the stock as collateral for a loan.

"It was the First Bank of Orange Crush or something, and Konsmo said he could place one hundred thousand dollars," Levy says. "He told us that would get us a forty-thousand-dollar loan."

"Why so small?" Levy demanded. "You ought to be able to get sixty thousand easy."

Konsmo said his banker didn't want to take any chances. "He'll lend us forty thousand dollars, and take five thousand off the top for himself. I'll take seventy-five hundred, and that'll leave twenty-seven thousand five hundred for you guys to divide up."

Levy decided it was time to ask Ernsten a few questions. "Everybody and his brother was getting in on our deal. We had no protection from the cops and no way to muscle these guys if they took our stock and went bye-bye." Ernsten told him not to worry. He reminded Levy of his contact in the FBI, and said he also belonged to a couple of powerful underground groups. One of the groups, he implied, had at least the tacit sponsorship of the FBI. "It had some screwball name—Snip, Scap and Scoop or something," Levy says. "Snipers-of-the-World, with a license to kill. It sounded crazy. He said if the FBI didn't like you and couldn't prove its case against you, they just had this group kill you. But if you think that was goofy, listen to this: Ernsten said he also belonged to the Hagannah." Levy couldn't restrain an "Oh, Jesus, here we go again" look when Ernsten said that, and he asked Ernsten, "The who?"

"The Hagannah. I am part of the people that smuggled out Eichmann."

"What the fuck are you talking about? You're not even Jewish."

"That doesn't mean anything. They worked with me. I—"

"You're a lunatic, you know. A real lunatic."

But Levy was desperate for money. He agreed to prepare $100,000 worth of stock for the Orange County banker and $2.5 million worth for Bo Farmer. They agreed to meet again later that week, either in Calaway's office or in a restaurant Calaway had just bought into.

"What's the restaurant?" Levy asked.

"Well, it's called the Scam, now, but—"

"The Scam?" Levy roared with laughter. He'd driven by the restaurant hundreds of times. It was a well-known spot on the west end of the Sunset Strip. But for this group to be meeting at a restaurant named the Scam was like Murder Inc. meeting at a restaurant called The Rub-Out.

Ernsten said they were going to change the name to the 9000 Club—the address of the restaurant (9000 Sunset Boulevard).

"No, no," Levy protested, still blinking back tears of laughter. "The Scam is perfect. It's priceless. Don't change it."

It was too late, Levy was told. The name-change had already been approved.

"Well then," Levy suggested, half-facetiously, "why don't we call ourselves 'The Nine Thousand Group.' That's a good code name."

To his astonishment, everyone agreed. In fact, they decided, Levy would henceforth be known as "The Beard," in acknowledgment of the black whiskers he was cultivating.

Levy went back to work preparing the stock. He included some International Industries, along with the International Chemical and Nuclear Corp., and when he was done, he arranged to deliver the stock to Iler—in a brown paper bag again. They met in front of the Beverly Rodeo Hyatt House—amid several of the poshest boutiques in Beverly Hills—and Levy turned over his paper sack. But when Farmer and Cox left for Phoenix, they went without the stock. At the last minute, it was decided they might both be recognized at the airport, and Ernsten didn't want to risk their having the stock if they were searched. Another man—John Dubeck, an ex-casino dealer from Las Vegas who also worked at the 9000 Club—was enlisted to make the actual delivery. He was to be paid $3,000 per trip plus $400 expenses. At night, the stock was transferred from the trunk of Ernsten's car to the trunk of Dubeck's car— while both were parked in the basement of the 9000 Club —and Dubeck, too, left for Phoenix.

When he arrived, he registered under an assumed name at a motel previously decided upon, paged Cox in the coffee shop and gave him the stock. On a hunch, Farmer checked the stock in the *Standard and Poor* stock guide and found that they had more than 10 percent of all outstanding shares in International Industries. They called Ernsten, and told him to have Levy provide some substitute stock. The stock was ready when Dubeck returned to Los Angeles, and on his next flight to Phoenix, he was to deliver the stock to someone waiting in front of the Hertz counter in the Phoenix airport. But his contact was late, and Dubeck hid the stock in a locker until he arrived. Then, that deal complete, he again flew back to Los Angeles.

At about the same time, Levy, Ryan and Iler were meeting on yet another deal. Iler said he owned a cannery in Turlock, a small northern California community of about 10,000 people, some eighty miles inland from San Francisco. The Hume Cannery was an established, successful business, Iler told Levy, and they were waiting for a letter of credit from a European bank. Iler wanted Levy to provide $900,-000 worth of stock on which they would borrow $600,-000, pending issuance of the letter of credit.

For some reason, Levy was a little uneasy about the deal.

"Turlock I didn't know from Tucumcari," he says, "and I couldn't figure how come they had to go to Europe for a loan. Besides, canneries aren't exactly my idea of big-money swindles, and we had too many little deals going anyway, too many people involved. I wanted to do a few ten-million-dollar deals and retire, not piddle away nine hundred thousand here and two hundred fifty thousand there and take forever to get rich."

But Levy still hadn't heard anything about the bigger deals with Tom Wilson and Mr. Todd. He decided he'd better get what he could where he could. He agreed to provide the stock, and he delivered it—as he had previously delivered the Phoenix stock—in a brown paper bag during a rendezvous in front of the Beverly Rodeo Hyatt House.

"I was to get 10 percent off the top, as soon as they made the loan, and they were going to pay the loan back in sixty days, when their European letter of credit came through. I figured the European letter of credit never existed. The whole thing was bullshit. But if they made the loan and gave me my ten percent—ninety thousand dollars —what did I care for canneries or letters of credit?"

The stock for the cannery loan, like the Phoenix stock, was entrusted to John Dubeck for delivery. Unbeknownst to Levy, the stock was actually being taken to Las Vegas for the loan. Dubeck's instructions: Roll the stock certificates up inside a newspaper, and give it to Iler in front of a liquor store on Sahara Avenue, near the Sahara Hotel. That's exactly what he did.

But Levy waited only two days, and when he hadn't heard from Gordon Iler, he went to see Ernsten. They got Iler on the telephone, and Iler said the loan was about to be made, and things were going smoothly.

"Don't shit me with your smoothly," Levy roared. "Everybody tells me everything's going smoothly, and meanwhile, I'm sitting here with no money. Things are going smoothly with Mr. Todd in Switzerland and things are going smoothly with Tom Wilson in London and things are going smoothly with Bo Farmer and those idiots in Phoenix and things are going smoothly with you in Turlock. Well, things ain't going smoothly with me. I've got almost ten million dollars' worth of stock out, and I still don't have a fuckin' penny to show for it."

He paused, his breath coming in short, angry bursts.

"Listen, I'm telling you, Gordon, if you come back to Los Angeles, come back with my money or my stock. Mr. Todd has my five million, Tom Wilson has one million, there's two-and-a-half million in Phoenix, and I'm not letting any more out. Get that? I don't have my stock, and I don't have my money. I want one or the other, Gordon. I want my stock back or I want my money. If you don't have one or the other, Gordon, don't bother coming back. Just don't come home."

He slammed the receiver down.

For all his threats and fulminations, Levy is not a violent man. He can, in fact, be a very gentle, tender man. He has never consciously inflicted physical pain on anyone, and he blanches at the mere thought of doing so. But at that particular point in time, he was about as close to actually throttling someone as he had ever been in his entire life. He left Ernsten's office in a blind rage, determined that someone was going to pay—and pay dearly—for all his aggravation.

When a few more days passed, and Levy hadn't heard anything about the Phoenix negotiations, he drove over to the 9000 Club, and asked Ernsten if Farmer was still in Phoenix.

"Sure, he and Ralph's friend, Cox, are at some big hotel there, the Camelback Inn or something. They—"

Levy cut in. "Big hotel? Who's paying for that?"

"It's expenses. He—"

"Your expenses, not mine!" Levy snapped.

Levy asked how soon they could expect their money;

Ernsten told him not to worry. He said he'd checked with his FBI contact recently, and "Everything's cool. No one even knows we exist."

Levy waited a day or two, then went back to the 9000 Club. By this time, Gerry Kassap was asking when he would be paid, and Levy was growing tired of stalling him off. He stormed in on his friends at the 9000 Club, and before they could say anything, he told them, "I don't give a shit what's going on. You get those assholes in Phoenix on the phone right now. I want to talk to them."

They gave Levy the telephone number of the hotel, and he called and asked for Farmer's room. When a woman answered and asked, "Who's calling?" Levy—in his own words—"went crazy."

"What the fuck do you mean, 'Who's calling?' Who the hell are you in my room?"

Startled by the outburst, she managed to stammer, "In your room? I'm in Mr. Farmer's room."

"Yeah, well who the fuck do you think is paying for Mr. Farmer's room—his rich old aunt in Scarsdale? Where is the son-of-a-bitch?"

The woman said he was "in conference."

"In conference? I suppose that means he's taking a crap. Well, you go tell him to get off the can and come to the phone."

The woman paused, and then said, "Well, actually, he's lying down in the sun, next to the pool."

Levy erupted again. "Lying in the sun? On my money? Look, bitch, do me a favor. You go out there and tell that asshole that Alan Levy called and he better call me back at the Nine Thousand Club. Now !" He hung up.

Thirty minutes later, Farmer called. Levy didn't give him a chance to get "hello" out of his mouth.

"What the fuck's going on there, you two-bit asshole? Where's my money? Where's Cox? What the hell's going on?"

Farmer said Cox was "in town."

"In town? He's in town and you're laying in the sun with a broad. What are you in Phoenix for anyway—a party? Physical therapy treatments? I don't understand it. You went there with two-and-a-half million dollars' worth of my stock, and you're having an orgy. I want my two hundred fifty thousand."

Farmer said he was "putting a deal together. I got a guy who's going to buy one hundred thousand dollars' worth of stock. He—"

Levy was so furious and dumbfounded, he could barely speak straight. "You got a who's gonna do what? Where'd you meet this *schmuck*?"

"On the street in—"

"On the street? What have you got, a corner haberdashery? A tie stand like King Levinsky? Where the hell's your brains, idiot? You can't peddle this stock like you're running a five-and-dime. You ain't Mr. Woolworth or Mrs. Newberry, jerk!"

But Farmer said he'd been introduced to the man "by the right people," and he was going to get $10,000 cash for the stock.

"That's just wonderful," Levy roared back. "Ten cents on the dollar. Bargain basement sales you're making yet." He stopped to catch his breath. "So when do we get this ten thousand?"

"In a day or two. I'm sending it back to L.A. with someone."

"Fine. Now get your ass in gear on the two-and-a-half million. And don't set up a corner stand to sell it either. You're not a kid selling ten-cent lemonade."

While waiting for that money—"Seems I'm always waiting for money, doesn't it?"—Levy got word that Ernsten wanted to see him in Martin Calaway's office. When he arrived, Ernsten looked frightened. Levy shuddered. "Oh, my God," he thought. "He heard from the FBI, and we're all going to jail."

"You know a lot of guys, don't you, Alan?" Ernsten asked.

"Yeah."

"Well, some guys from Palm Springs are after me. Big guys. Mafia guys."

Levy rolled his eyes. "I was getting tired of hearing Mafia already. But Ernsten was obviously scared. All of a sudden, he wasn't so calm and cool, talking all about the FBI and Snip, Scap and Scoop and the Hagannah anymore. He was shitting in his pants, and he wanted me to sit in on a meeting with these guys. When I saw how they worked him over, I could understand why. They were tough. Apparently, Ernsten had shafted them on some deal, and they weren't going to sit still for it. I don't know what I was supposed to do about it, and I never heard about those guys again."

But the next day—to Levy's immense surprise and delight—the $10,000 Farmer had promised him from the first Phoenix deal arrived in Los Angeles. He went to Martin Calaway's office for his cut—$5,000. "Not exactly eight hundred million, but when you'd had your *putz* pulled as long as I had, you're grateful for almost anything." Almost is right. When Levy got to Calaway's office, Ernsten was there. "You get a check for one thousand, two hundred fifty dollars," he said.

"What do you mean one thousand, two hundred fifty dollars?" Levy asked.

"Well, that's half of twenty-five hundred."

"What happened to the other seventy-five hundred?"

"Expenses."

"Expenses? You gotta be kidding. What expenses?"

"The plane tickets, the hotel rooms, the food, the—"

"Get out of here. You could spend a month in Europe on seventy-five hundred dollars. You couldn't blow seventy-five hundred in Phoenix if you had a year to do it."

"Well, I can show you the bills. They—"

"No, don't show me the bills. You show me the bills and it'll come out that *I* owe *you* one thousand two hundred fifty dollars."

"Take it easy, Alan. Remember, the seventy-five hundred dollars expenses should cover everything on the Phoenix deal. When we get our two hundred fifty thousand, it'll be all profit."

"And when do we get the two hundred fifty thousand?"

"Soon."

Levy shrugged, picked up his check and left. He figured he'd already spent a few thousand dollars on plane tickets and stamps and pens and phone calls himself—not to mention the time he'd invested that probably could have been better spent making money from another scheme or two; he decided he wouldn't even tell Steve Berg and Gerry Kassap about the $1,250 check: "In my pocket, with a bip and a bop and a boop."

That was on a Wednesday. On Friday morning, in Calaway's office, Levy gave Ernsten $100,000 worth of stock for Finn Konsmo to place with his friendly banker in Orange County. That night, Konsmo drove his pickup truck to the Airport Marina Hotel, and left it in the parking lot —unlocked. While he was inside the hotel, killing time, Ernsten drove up, threw the stock in on the floor of the pickup, locked the door and drove away. Konsmo returned to the pickup and drove it home. On Monday, Ernsten called him to confirm all the arrangements.

The following Friday, Konsmo took the stock to his banker, and made the prearranged $40,000 loan. Late that same afternoon, he brought six cashier's checks back to Calaway's office. He'd already taken his out, he said; so had the banker. He had individual checks made out in his name for all the others, and he would endorse the checks over to them. Everyone agreed except Levy. He was supposed to get $10,000 to divide with Steve Berg and Gerald Kassap, but he didn't want his share in a check.

"No way my name was going on the back of any check," he says. "I had them go to the savings and loan downstairs to cash one of the checks and give me five thousand dollars in cash—all in one-hundred-dollar bills. The other five-thousand-dollar check, endorsed by Konsmo, I agreed to take."

When Levy left Calaway's office, he called Kassap, and arranged a meeting outside Nibbler's Coffee Shop in Beverly Hills. "I've got a check for you," Levy told him, "so be cool. Try not to be too obvious." Levy was wasting his breath. "This coffee shop is in a pretty nice spot, just off Wilshire Boulevard and Santa Monica Boulevard, with a lot of nice shops and professional offices all around. So how does my suave co-conspirator be cool and unobtrusive? He drives up to Nibbler's in a *farkokte* camper—a great big white camper you could only spot from three hundred and fifty miles away."

Levy gave Kassap the $5,000 check, then called Steve Berg. Conveniently forgetting the $5,000 cash he'd just pocketed, he told Berg, "We only got five thousand dollars, and I gave it all to Gerry to keep him quiet. There's plenty more where that came from. You and I can take our cut out of the next deal."

But instead of another deal, an intermediary for Tom Wilson called Levy, and said Wilson had been unable to make his loan in London. A banker there had suggested checking the stock with the transfer agent in New York, the intermediary said, and Wilson had panicked. "He took the stock back, ran out of the bank and buried everything under a coal pile somewhere."

Levy didn't know whether to believe the story or not, and after spending the better part of two days on the tennis club telephone, he still wasn't certain. In between calls trying to track down Wilson, he placed calls to Ernsten and Farmer and his other partners. But everything was at a standstill. He walked home more disconsolately after each futile round of calls.

Chapter 4

A couple of days later, an old friend stopped by Levy's house. The man's name was "Fats" Jackson, a five-foot-five-inch, 350-pound hustler who had been in business with Levy at various times. They had owned a restaurant together, started their own luggage store, backed a pillow-manufacturing plant. Together, the two had been quite a pair—two blustery flim-flam men brimming with schemes for swindling the world.

"The pillow company was our best one," Levy says. "I remember one time when our supplier refused to send us an order of fabric to make our pillows, just because we were a few thousand dollars behind in paying them for the last shipment. Well, Fats called them on the phone and started screaming like a mad man. How dare they not fill our order! How dare they question our credit! Why, we had one hundred thousand dollars' worth of orders from J.C. Penney on hand at that very moment. While Fats is talking, a salesman from the fabric company walks in. Fats picks up a fistful of last year's orders from J.C. Penney, and he yells 'Alan, isn't this one hundred thousand dollars' worth of orders from J.C. Penney?' I look at him: 'Damn right it is,' I yell back, loud enough for them to hear me over the phone. Then I jerk the orders out of his hand and wave them in the salesman's face. 'Isn't this one hundred thousand dollars' worth of orders from J.C. Penney?' I ask, practically breathing down his throat. 'Well, yes, I guess so,' he stammers. 'Then get on the phone,' I tell him. 'Tell that goddamn company of yours to ship our fabric, or we'll take our business elsewhere.' The fabric arrived before the week was out."

Levy and Fats Jackson weren't always that successful —or that happy together—but they remained on good terms and kept in touch with one another through the years. On this particular day, Jackson was just stopping by to see how Levy was doing. Levy decided to have a little fun with him. He took out a big handful of the $100 bills he'd gotten in the Finn Konsmo payoff, and began throwing them wildly all over the living room, chanting, "Money, Fats, money, money, money. Look at all of it."

Jackson was practically slobbering in his eagerness for the details: "Where did you get it? Where did it come from? How much have you got? How much is there?"

When Jackson stopped babbling, Levy told him the whole story, and asked if he knew anyone who might be able to use the stock to their mutual advantage. Jackson said he would ask around. A few days later, he came back. "I know a doctor. I think he can help us."

On his next visit, Jackson brought the good doctor with him. Again, Levy went through the explanation of where the stock came from and how he got it. The doctor said he had a friend who knew a banker in the San Fernando Valley, just northwest of downtown Los Angeles. He also had a friend who could "dump millions and millions of dollars' worth in Switzerland." But "millions" was no longer a magic word for Alan Levy. If anything, it was a dirty word. "Look," he told the doctor, "I won't bore you with all the gory details, but I've been involved in deals for millions for the last three or four months, and I'm still waiting for my money. Don't try to impress me with your millions. Let's just do one deal at a time, doc. How much stock can you use now—right now?"

"Say two hundred thousand dollars' worth. We can probably borrow—"

"I don't care what you can borrow. I don't care who or how or where. I already got so many deals going, I don't know where the fuck I am. I'm so confused, I wake up some mornings, and I can't find my own ass with both hands. All I want to know is how much stock you need. All you gotta know is I get ten percent off the top every time you make a loan. You want two hundred thousand dollars now? Fine. I get twenty thousand. Cut and dried. Simple. Okay? I don't get my twenty thousand tomorrow or next week or later. I get it up front the minute you make the loan. And I'm going to the bank with you. I give you the stock. You go inside. I wait outside. You come back out and give me my twenty thousand dollars and I give Fats five thousand of that for finding you. Got it?"

The doctor nodded.

"Good," Levy said. "When do you want it and who do you want it made out to?"

"Put it in the name of Irving Davis."

"Who's that?"

"It's a name I use sometimes. See?" With that, he pulled out a whole sheaf of credit cards issued to Irving Davis.

Levy prepared the stock, put it in a paper bag and went to meet the doctor at a coffee shop in nearby Van Nuys. The plan was for the doctor to call his friend from the coffee shop, and the three men would rendezvous at the bank. But when Levy arrived at the coffee shop, the doctor said his friend—"Frank," he called him—couldn't make it. Frank, he said, was in Israel. The doctor suggested that Levy give him the stock anyway—"to get things going. When Frank returns, in a day or two, we can meet again."

Levy laughed. "What do you think I am, crazy? No tickee, no laundry. I told you, I'm not giving you the stock until we're ready to walk into the bank and get the money."

The doctor persisted. Finally, Levy said, "Okay, look,

you buy me two round-trip tickets to Europe as a sort of down payment, and I'll leave the stock with you."

The idea had hit Levy suddenly; if he got to Europe, he might be able to track down Tom Wilson and Mr. Todd. At the very least, he could treat his wife to a much-deserved vacation while they were waiting for more money to roll in. Or, failing that, he could always cash the tickets in for some spending money in L.A.

But the doctor wouldn't buy the tickets. "Meet me here again tomorrow," he said. "Maybe Frank will be back by then."

They met and still no Frank. Again, the doctor asked Levy to give him the stock. Again, Levy asked for two round-trip tickets to Europe. This time, the doctor agreed.

That night—actually, it was one o'clock in the morning—Levy and the doctor met at Los Angeles International Airport. They booked passage for Levy and his wife two days hence from Los Angeles to London to Dusseldorf to Zurich to Paris and back—a ten-day trip, costing $1,650. Levy gave the doctor the stock, with explicit instructions to give his $20,000 to Fats Jackson as soon as the loan transaction was completed.

The next day, Fred Ryan came by to see Levy again. Keith Simpson—who had been present at one of the early meetings with Ernsten and Iler—had a line on a good deal, Ryan said. He wanted to see Levy right away. That night, Levy, Ryan and Simpson met at the airport. Simpson knew a banker in Zurich, he said, and as long as Levy was going there, they ought to get together. "He can do us a lot of good," Simpson said. "He can place two hundred fifty thousand dollars' worth of stock at a time, in regular incre-ments, as much as you got. His name is George Alpo."

"Wonderful," Levy said. "Just what I need now—a banker who specializes in dog food."

But Simpson was serious. "Your contacts will be a Herr Ludwig Hellmer, a German, and a Mr. Leonard Bernstein, an American. They'll be in Dusseldorf. Why don't you meet them there. If you want, I'll call them now."

When Simpson placed the call, Levy understood why he had suggested meeting at the airport. It seems that Simpson had drilled a hole in the coin box of one of the telephones there, and he could insert an instrument in the hole and get all his money back, no matter where he called. The phone booth had become his regular office, and his ingenious little device was supposed to impress Levy. Instead, it had just the opposite effect. "Here we were," Levy says, "talking about multimillion-dollar deals with Swiss banks, and I got a partner who has to drill holes in public telephones so he can afford to make a phone call."

Simpson called Dusseldorf, and arranged for Levy to meet Hellmer and Bernstein there. They wanted to know how they would recognize Levy. "Just tell them I'm short, fat and Jewish, with a beard, long hair and glasses. If there's two people who look like that in the Dusseldorf airport at the same time, we're all in trouble."

Levy had made every effort to keep his wife, Frannie, in the dark about most of his shady dealings. He didn't want to frighten her or risk involving her, so he was as vague as possible about what he was doing. She was an astonishingly naive woman—"twenty-six going on fourteen," is the way one friend described her—and she seemed to adhere to the philosophy that if she ignored any trouble, it would go away. If anyone asked her what her husband did for a living, she said he was a financier. She paid no attention to anything that would contradict that answer and rarely asked questions. When Levy suddenly announced they were going to Europe for ten days, "to have some fun and work on that movie deal I told you about," she was delighted and not the least bit suspicious or inquisitive. Her only concern was their baby girl, Nicole, and Levy persuaded her to leave Nicole with her grandmother —Frannie's mother—though Levy was actually even more reluctant to leave Nicole behind than Frannie was. For all his finagling and his tough-guy exterior, Levy has always been a devoted father. That is especially true with Nicole; he dotes on her more than the most stereotypically attentive Jewish mother. Being apart from her for even a day worries him, and to leave her for ten days—"Well," he says, "if things hadn't been so desperate, I never would have left. But we had to break loose one of those deals. I was tired of not being able to give the baby the right food, and I was already thinking of how I would buy her clothes and cars and send her to college and all."

Levy and his wife took a 747 to London, leaving all the stock behind. For Levy, this was to be essentially a scouting mission. He would look up Tom Wilson's friend, Mario Denard, in London, meet with Leonard Bernstein and Ludwig Hellmer in Dusseldorf and, hopefully, arrange a deal with Keith Simpson's banker friend, Alpo, in Zurich. While he was in Zurich, he'd try to get to Paris for a few days, so Frannie could see the sights. Then, if everything worked out, he'd come home, pick up some stock and return to Europe to consummate whatever transactions he was able to arrange on this first trip.

As soon as he landed in London, Levy telephoned Mario Denard. Denard gave him his address, and suggested he take a cab over.

"Tom Wilson had told me he was a very rich guy with a beautiful apartment and a lot of influence, so I figured it was okay to take Frannie there. Shit! His apartment looked like a brownstone walk-up in New York. Nothing special, nothing fancy. And Denard? He comes to the door in his undershirt, looking like Marlon Brando in *A Streetcar Named Desire*, but without the sex appeal. Just your typical, everyday slob. He was living with some girl, and she was ironing his shirts. A real floozy, she was. Like, if she was a hundred-dollar hooker, you'd want ninety-nine dollars and ninety-nine cents change. Well, I sit down with Denard, and right away, I know he couldn't finance a second-hand pickup truck, let alone a million-dollar movie."

Denard said he had hidden the stock Levy had given to Tom Wilson. It was "safe, under a coal pile," and he wanted to know what Levy wanted to do with it.

"Hold it for a few days. I gotta go to Dusseldorf and maybe Zurich. No sense in me carting the stuff all over the continent. I'll stop here on my way back to the States, and pick it up then."

They shook hands, and Levy ushered his wife outside. He felt guilty about having subjected her to the tawdry scene in Denard's apartment, so he suggested they go shopping for a few hours before flying on to Dusseldorf. On the way to Harrod's department store, they got into an argument; Frannie wanted to stay overnight in London, but Levy had to meet Hellmer and Bernstein that afternoon in Dusseldorf. Frannie started crying and walked across the street, away from her husband. He followed her and tried to reason with her. Just then, a would-be Sir Galahad walked over and accused him of "trying to pick up this young lady." Before Levy could explain, the stranger turned to Frannie and said, "Is this fellow bothering you?"

Levy spluttered in indignation: "This is my wife, you asshole. Get the fuck out of here. Mind your own friggin' business."

The stranger, dumbfounded, walked quickly away, and the Levys strolled into Harrod's, where they resumed their argument. Again, Frannie left Alan.

"Now, I'm really getting mad. I want to be unobtrusive, just in case Scotland Yard or Freddie, Bernie and Irving know what I'm up to, and I almost get arrested on the street for molesting my own wife. Now I have to get into arguments in the middle of the biggest department store in the whole world. Not only that, but she gets lost. The one thing I don't want to do is go to the police, but how else am I going to find her? For two hours, I walk up and down every aisle and up and down every floor. Finally, I decide, screw it, I'm gonna get some lunch. Then I'll go to the American embassy, and have them put out an all-points bulletin—'One dipshit American lady running around loose.' "

Levy walked down the street to a small restaurant, and who was sitting at the counter? His wife. They made up and ate lunch and headed for the airport. Frannie—exhausted from the argument and tension, and not yet adjusted to the transatlantic time-change—dozed off the minute they boarded the plane. But Levy's adrenalin was still pumping. He was also afraid; as a Jew whose family talked at great length about the Nazi atrocities when he was growing up, he was more than a little apprehensive about going to Germany. Intellectually, he knew there was no reason, in 1971, for his fear. Emotionally . . . well, that was another story.

When they landed in Dusseldorf, a jeep filled with security guards came out to meet the plane—a routine practice at many European airports. But Levy didn't know that, and he was petrified. "Either someone squealed on the stock deal, or they found out I'm a Jew," he thought. "Either way, I'm a dead man. Dachau here I come."

After a thorough search at Customs—"Thank God, I didn't bring any stock with me"—Levy started looking around for Ludwig Hellmer and Leonard Bernstein. He waited and waited and waited, but no one showed up. Then he heard his name over the airport public address system: "Herr Levy. Come to the B.E.A. ticket counter, please. Herr Levy." That shattered what little remained of his equilibrium: "What kind of maniacs am I dealing with anyway? We're crooks, swindlers, don't they know that? We're supposed to sneak in and out of foreign countries using aliases and disguises. We're not supposed to be paging each other in the airport. We might as well throw an autograph party, and give out free samples of our stock to all the local cops."

Levy waited a few minutes, then walked furtively toward the B.E.A. ticket counter. "I'm Herr Levy," he whispered. He was handed a message: *Unable to meet plane. Come to the Intercontinental Hotel. Will contact you there. Assad.* "So who's Assad? I was waiting for Hellmer and Bernstein." Levy decided the message was a warning that the police had found them out. But he had nothing else to do, so he and Frannie checked into the Intercontinental.

As they walk into the hotel, they can't help noticing a crowd of about thirty people, screaming and shouting in German at one American. The American seems reasonably calm, considering that he seems about to be lynched; he's telling the crowd, "Please wait. Just be calm. Everything will be all right. I can explain."

Levy figured that given his previous experience with the stock, the American had to be Bernstein. But he wasn't about to go strolling into that angry mob and introduce himself, so he and Frannie just checked into their room.

An hour later, they still hadn't heard from Assad or Hellmer or Bernstein or anyone else. "You know, Frannie," Levy said, "why don't we go out to dinner and go to bed, and if no one calls by tomorrow, we'll just head for Paris." That, she said, was the best news she'd heard all year.

But while they were changing clothes and cleaning up for dinner, the telephone rang. It was Assad. He said he was calling for Bernstein and Hellmer, and he wanted to see Levy in the hotel cocktail lounge at eight o'clock that night. Levy agreed. "You stay in the room," he told Frannie. "I'll come back up for you as soon as I know what's going on down there."

At eight o'clock sharp, Levy took the elevator down to the lobby and walked casually into the cocktail lounge. At one end of the bar, he saw six people—including the American he'd seen surrounded by Germans in the lobby a few hours earlier. The American was in his early forties, very distinguished looking. He was an inch or so under six feet, slender, with brown eyes and collar-length, dark-brown hair tinged with gray at the temples. He was certainly no dead-ringer for the *real* Leonard Bernstein, but his general appearance was sufficiently similar that someone who didn't know the maestro on sight probably would automatically assume this was he, especially after hearing him speak. Born in Philadelphia, Bernstein spoke a smooth, well-cultured English. His drinking companions were two men —a German and an Arab—and three women. The German looked to be in his early sixties (he was actually about ten years younger) and he, too, was tall and slender. He was only an inch or so taller than Bernstein, but because he stood ramrod-straight, he looked even taller. His features were distinctly Aryan, from his blue eyes to his aquiline nose and rigid posture, but his hair, incongruously, was jet-black. Like Bernstein, he seemed nervous, fidgety. Both men were drumming their fingers on the bar and twitching their necks, seemingly trying to look both ways at once. The Arab with them was in his mid-forties. He had dark eyes, dark hair and an olive complexion. Levy figured him for a Lebanese. The Arab was the only one of the six who wasn't drinking, and judging from their glazed eyes and sloppy demeanor, Levy gauged that the other five had more than made up for what he'd missed. But what really caught Levy's eye was another man, at the opposite end of the bar.

"He was the stereotypical Nazi," Levy recalls. "Tall, blond, blue eyes, standing at attention like the bartender was a general and this was full dress inspection. Fresh from the Gestapo for sure."

As Levy walked in, the olive-skinned man saw him and walked over. "You're Levy?" Levy nodded. "Good. I'm Assad." Then he introduced Levy to Bernstein and Hellmer. At that moment, the German at the other end of the bar said something to the bartender. "He said 'The Americans are too noisy,'" Hellmer translated for Bernstein, and Bernstein whirled and shouted, "Hey, you Nazi son-of-a-bitch. Shoot your mouth off again, and I'll bust a beer bottle over your skull." Levy cringed. "In the first place, the guy was right. With all they'd been drinking, they *were* noisy. And even if they weren't, you don't go threatening to bust up guys when you're in a bar in their country—especially not if the country's Germany and your names are Bernstein and Levy."

Before the "secret" meeting could degenerate into a barroom brawl, the German left. A few minutes later, Assad took Levy by the arm, and walked him into the lobby. "I don't think those two guys are sober enough to talk business tonight."

Levy had a sinking sensation in the pit of his still-empty stomach. "Here I was, a Jew in Germany, dealing with an Arab and two drunks."

He excused himself for a moment. "My wife and I were just going to have dinner. Let me tell her I've been detained."

Still grumbling to himself, Levy walked to a house telephone and called his room. "I'm sorry, Frannie, but we're not going to be able to eat together. Two of these jerks are drunk and the third one thinks he's Nasser. It looks like I'm gonna be stuck down here awhile trying to figure things out. Why don't you go ahead and order dinner for yourself in the room. I'll be up later."

Frannie said she'd do that, and Levy returned to Assad. Cautiously, he asked the Arab how he'd gotten involved in the stock deal.

"Oh, I'm just passing through."

Levy nodded dumbly, then decided to try again: "What do you do?"

Assad brightened considerably. "I make gold coins."

"Where?"

"In Beirut. In my garage."

"Oh, counterfeit?"

"No, real gold coins. We stamp old dates on new coins to make them look rare. Then we smuggle them into the United States, through Mexico, and sell them."

"Oh." Assad, he thought, should be named Asshole.

Just then, Assad launched into a long, rambling account of how he had picked up the girl he was with in the bar. Levy, hungry and fatigued by the five-hour time difference, wasn't much interested in Assad's tales of sexual conquest, and Assad seemed to sense that. After telling Levy about "a special little trick" his girl was going to perform for him in the bathtub in his room, he abruptly changed subjects and started to explain how he had met Bernstein. But Levy was too thoroughly bewildered and disgusted by then to care.

"Are you going to be meeting with us tomorrow on the stock deal?" he asked.

"No. I'm flying to Beirut tomorrow."

"Well, what the fuck is going on then? I fly halfway around the world on a multimillion-dollar deal, and they're drunk and you're going to Beirut?"

Unseen by either man, Bernstein had walked over during the conversation, and he told Levy, in alcohol-slurred tones, "Don't worry about anything. Why don't you get a good night's sleep, and you and Ludwig and I can straighten this all out tomorrow."

It was after ten o'clock by this time, and Levy was not at all averse to a little sleep. Bernstein said he or Hellmer would call him in the morning. Everyone said goodnight, and Levy took the elevator to his room. Frannie, he noticed, was already sleeping soundly. Good, he thought. Poor kid's probably dead-tired. So am I. He took off his clothes and was asleep in minutes. At midnight, the telephone rang. It was Steve Berg in Los Angeles and he was angry. A friend had told him that Levy had bought his wife $1,500 worth of clothes and took off for Europe. That must mean one of their big stock deals came through. Berg wants his share. Groggily, Levy tries to explain about Tom Wilson and Mr. Todd and the doctor and Bo Farmer and Bernstein and Assad and. . . . Suddenly, he realizes he's talking on a hotel telephone, across the transatlantic cable, and the conversation could easily be monitored. He tries to terminate the conversation. Berg demands a full accounting. Finally, Levy says, "Goddamn it, Steve, everybody and his brother could be listening to this. Why don't you just take out an ad in *The Times:* 'Hot stock for sale.' Maybe you could buy a billboard on the Sunset Strip better. Now get off the goddamn phone. When I have something to report, I'll report. Don't worry, no one's cheating you." After almost an hour on the phone, Levy just hung up.

He woke up surprisingly well-rested the next morning, and he and Frannie had breakfast in their room—"a typical German breakfast, you know, eighty-two pounds of meat, thirty-five rolls, hot potato salad and coffee so strong you could either get drunk on it or use it to flush the radiator in your car."

After breakfast, Frannie said she missed the baby and wanted to go home. She didn't ask Levy a single question about his meetings the previous night. As usual, she didn't want to know anything that might make her the least bit uncomfortable or apprehensive. What she didn't know, she must have figured, couldn't hurt her. Levy ignored her complaint about missing their daughter, and didn't volunteer any information about his conversation with Assad. He'd been married to Frannie long enough to know what she did and didn't want to hear. Munching on a roll, he picked up the telephone and asked for Bernstein's room. No answer. "Come on, honey, let's go for a walk," he said. They walked along the Rhine for a while, then took a cab downtown, where Alan bought his wife a beautiful pair of brown boots. After a leisurely lunch of "the best goulash I ever had," they returned to the hotel in good spirits.

"It was a beautiful spring day—seventy or seventy-five

degrees, with bright sunshine—and all the people were friendly as could be. We saw boats going up and down the river, and just had a marvelous time."

Once back in the hotel, he called Bernstein's room.

"Who's this?" Bernstein asked.

"Alan Levy."

"Who?"

"What do you mean who? Alan Levy. Keith Simpson's friend. We met last night. Or were you too drunk to remember?"

"Oh." Pause. "*That* Alan Levy."

"Why, you know any other Alan Levys in Dusseldorf today?"

Bernstein said he was in the process of checking out and moving to a smaller hotel, the Esplanade, downtown. He said he'd call Levy back in an hour or so. Levy hung up, furious. "I got an Arab who's probably left the country, Bernstein checking out of the hotel and God knows where Hellmer is." When Bernstein called back, it was to suggest a dinner date for that night—"you and your wife, Ludwig and his wife and me and my girl friend." Levy agreed.

Over dinner, Bernstein said he was an architect. Hellmer said he was a scientist. Levy's wife was duly impressed. Levy wasn't. But Bernstein told them all about Hellmer. Hellmer, he said, was drafted into the Wehrmacht during World War II. "He didn't want to fight for the Nazis—"

Levy, his voice crackling with sarcasm, interrupted him. "Amazing. No one wanted to fight for the Nazis. They had eight million cards out to deaf, dumb and blind people." Just before he'd left the United States, Levy had been listening to a folk song about the post-war German campaign to obliterate the Nazi image, and now he sang a few of the lyrics:

"Each and every German dances to the strain
Of the 'I was not a Nazi polka'
All without exception join in the refrain

Of the 'I was not a Nazi polka'
Goring was a crazy we wanted to deport
I was not a Nazi polka
We all thought that Dachau was just a nice resort
I was not a Nazi polka ..."*

But Bernstein wouldn't tolerate Levy's bitterness—or
his "rudeness." Levy, he said, was paranoid; Hellmer was
a good man—a man so unhappy with having to fight for the
Nazis that he had deliberately shot himself in the leg. But
before he could be shipped back to a hospital behind the
lines, he was captured by the Russians, and imprisoned
near Stalingrad for nine years.

The story reminded Levy of his own military experience.
Like Hellmer, he hadn't exactly been a gung-ho soldier.
He'd enlisted in the Air Force during the Korean War to
avoid being drafted after he'd dropped out of school during his first semester at the University of Illinois. A compulsive and delightfully entertaining storyteller, he decided
to share the tale of his abortive military exploits with his
dinner companions.

"It didn't take long for me to realize I wasn't cut out to
be a military hero," he told them. "The first night in my
barracks at basic training, I fall asleep, and all of a sudden,
I hear a fuckin' bugle. I was up like a shot. I was sure the
fuckin' Chinese were coming over the hill. I jerk my uniform on and race outside, and it's cold and dark and I can't
see my hand in front of me.

"Then some jerk starts calling roll.

" 'Jones.'

" 'Here.'

" 'Williamson.'

" 'Here.'

" 'Fredericks.'

" 'Here.'

" 'Levy.'

"I don't answer.

" 'Levy.'

"I still don't answer.

" 'Private Alan Charles Levy.' "

Disgustedly—shivering in the mid-February chill—Levy mutters, "I'm here. Where the hell else would I be?"

The drill sergeant says, "Take one step forward."

Levy looks at the row of men directly in front of him. "If I do, I'm gonna step on this guy's heels."

"What did you say, private?"

"Look, what is this anyway? It must be four o'clock in the morning. It's so dark, I can't see my own fly. I'm so cold, my teeth sound like castanets. I don't even know where I am, and you want to know if I'm here. You got a barbed wire fence around this place. Where would I go? What'd you even wake me up for? To say 'Here'? Do we go to breakfast now and start our training or what?"

"No," the sergeant explained. "Chow is at seven."

"You got to be kidding me. You mean to tell me you woke us up and pulled us out here in the middle of the night just to count us?"

"This is roll call and reveille, private."

"Who-call and what-a-lee?"

And that, Levy told his companions, was "my introduction to the United States Air Force."

Everyone—even Hellmer—was laughing. Levy decided to finish the story.

"I started poring through the military manual, looking for any way out. I thought of shooting a toe off, feigning homosexuality, fainting—anything. Even the food was getting to me.

"My first meal was a chicken they must have chased all the way across Texas. The second meal I got powdered milk—powdered milk? What did I need that for? Well, I tried. At the third meal, I even filled my plate all the way up. But I couldn't finish it. This big Southern sergeant comes up behind me and says, 'Y'all eat what's on yo' plate, heah?' I ate it."

A couple of weeks after his enlistment, Levy went out on bivouac—"all spiffed out in a new uniform that made me look like some half-assed Greyhound bus driver." Asthmatic since childhood, he'd heard that asthmatics were often placed on limited service during World War II, and he was determined to have a bad asthma attack on bivouac. He brought a couple of cigars along from the PX, and two miles out, during a rest stop in a swirling dust storm, he pulled a blanket over his head and started smoking one— inhaling the smoke like a beached marlin. He even asked a friend to flap the blanket back and forth to allow some dust to mingle with the smoke.

"Needless to say, I collapsed. They took me to the hospital in a jeep, and gave me some kind of *farkokte* medicine I was allergic to. But I recovered, and they had me back on duty in three days. Wouldn't you know it—the next test is where they put you in a room with tear gas and make you take your gas masks off and file out slowly, so you can get a taste of what it's like. Wonderful. Just what I always wanted to taste. I flipped my mask off the minute they turned the gas on. If that didn't give me a fatal asthma attack, I figured nothing would. By the time I filed out with the rest of the guys, I collapsed again. Back to the hospital. But I was really bad this time. I got an oxygen tent and everything. What they didn't do to me . . . forget about it."

Shortly after he recovered, Levy was discharged. "My Air Force career lasted exactly thirty-four days."

The entire table was in stitches. Even their waiter had lingered long enough to catch the flavor of the story, and he, too, was laughing. After a little more small talk, Bernstein mentioned something about the stock Levy stared him into silence. Hellmer, he noticed, had been taking notes on almost everything that was said. The only time he'd stopped writing was when he was doubled over with laughter during Levy's story about his Air Force days.

Levy looked at Bernstein. "Why is Ludwig taking notes? Who the hell appointed him class secretary? Ever since we sat down, he's been scribbling on that little pad. Don't tell me he's just practicing his shorthand either."

Hellmer protested that he wasn't making notes secretly; he was writing on the table, where everyone could see.

"I don't care if you're writing in the toilet," Levy countered. "I just want to know why you're taking notes at all. If there's one thing we don't need, it's a nice, neat, written record for the cops to find."

Hellmer explained that he meant no harm. "I'm just a very systematic person. That's the way German people are. Very organized and systematic. This way, we will have a record of everything everyone says, and we can go back to it if we have any disagreements."

"That," Levy said, "we can very easily do without."

But Hellmer, oblivious to either the force or logic of Levy's argument, continued blithely on, writing down everything that was said, even though the conversation was mostly idle chitchat.

"You don't talk about multimillion-dollar swindles in a public restaurant with three women around," Levy hissed into Bernstein's ear when he suggested they "get down to business" over cognac after dinner.

The meal was superb, though, and the three women got along well, and Bernstein said he and Hellmer would pick Levy up at his hotel the next morning and take him to meet a friend who would help them dispose of some stock.

"The dog-food man?" Levy asked.

"No, he's out of the picture. This guy's better."

The next morning, when Bernstein and Hellmer came to the hotel, Bernstein brought a ring, a present for Frannie. She was delighted. "See," she told her husband, "I told you

he was a high-class guy." Levy just grumbled to himself:
"Exactly what I need—a bullshit artist giving me a jerk-
off routine and trying to get into my wife's pants with a
dime-store crackerjack ring."

As they left the hotel, Hellmer told Levy a little about
the man they were going to meet. He was known, Hellmer
said, as the Baron and he'd been a much-decorated soldier
in the French Indochina War. He'd fought at Dienbienphu
and he'd won the Legion of Honor and he was a genuine
war hero in France. He'd even been elected to some office. Then, in the early 1960's, he'd somehow gotten involved with master art forger Elmyr de Hory—the man
Clifford Irving wrote the book *Fake!* about—and he'd
fallen into national disgrace. He was a fugitive from several countries, Hellmer said, but he'd made several valuable contacts while he was working with de Hory, and he
was interested in talking to them about the stock.

Levy, Hellmer and Bernstein arrived at the Baron's small
apartment on the outskirts of Dusseldorf shortly before
noon, and Hellmer made all the introductions. Levy liked
the Baron immediately.

"I don't know why, there was just something about him,
he and I fell in love right away. He was a big guy, about
six foot, maybe two hundred and seventy, two hundred
and eighty pounds, with a huge belly. His mother was
French and his father was Italian, and those were the only
languages he spoke—which wouldn't have been so bad, I
guess, except that the broad he was living with was German, and she couldn't speak French or Italian. I don't
know how the hell they talked to each other."

Levy, a brilliant mimic, has a facility for *sounding* as if
he can speak almost any foreign language. His mastery
of tone and accent and dialect and inflection border on
genius. He can mix three or four French words—or Italian
words or German words or Russian words—into an otherwise thoroughly English conversation, put the proper for-

eign accent on all the words (English *and* foreign), and almost make you think he's speaking the foreign language fluently. But he doesn't really speak—or understand—*any* foreign language, and that made communication especially difficult in the Baron's apartment.

"Me and Leonard speak only English. The Baron speaks French and Italian. The broad he's living with speaks only German. And we're trying to negotiate a complicated international swindle. Of course, Ludwig speaks German. So he and the Baron's old lady can talk to each other all day. Wonderful. The two of them can talk, and he can take notes and the rest of us can smile and make faces at each other."

Fortunately, Hellmer also spoke a little French, and, somehow—between sips of champagne—everyone managed to give everyone else at least a vague idea of what they were about that morning. The Baron said he had an English friend who could help them dispose of the stock in large quantities, and they arranged to meet again—with him —at the Dusseldorf Hilton the next afternoon. But Levy and the Baron liked each other so well, they all decided to have dinner together that night.

At one o'clock the next afternoon, Levy, Hellmer and Bernstein drove to the Hilton. As they pulled into the open-air parking lot, they saw a new, royal-blue Cadillac convertible pull in.

"It was the Baron, of course," Levy says. "Another inconspicuous car for our entourage—a royal blue Cadillac convertible in Dusseldorf."

Stumbling through the language barrier, the Baron introduced the three men to his English friend, John Davidson, who owned the Cadillac. The five of them went into the hotel.

"We had our own United Nations right there," Levy says, "a German, two American Jews, an Englishman, and a half-French, half-Italian war hero. And we're all wearing suits, right? Like we're going to a state funeral or something."

The men rejected the hotel cocktail lounge as a place to talk—"It was too dark; if we couldn't understand each other, at least we wanted to see each other"—and they finally settled into a small sitting room off the lobby. After Levy explained the origin of his stock, Davidson started talking, in very clipped, very proper British tones. He had an associate, he said, who was a member of one of the most prominent families in all of England. "The governor," as he called him, owned a bank in Luxembourg, and had connections throughout the international banking community.

"What's his name?" Levy asked.

"I don't believe I'm at liberty to tell you just yet," Davidson replied.

"Oh, oh," Levy thought. "Another one of those. He thinks he's gonna take my stock and a zip and a zap and away he goes."

"Let's get something straight right away," Levy said. "I get twenty percent of the action, up front. You want one hundred thousand dollars' worth of stock, I get twenty thousand. You want a million dollars' worth of stock, I get two hundred thousand. Okay?"

"Well," Davidson said, "I'll have to check with the governor."

"Fine. You just do that."

Throughout the meeting, Levy had noticed Hellmer occasionally nudging Bernstein and nodding toward a man sitting in the corner. When everyone disappeared, Levy took Bernstein aside and asked for an explanation.

"You aren't the only one who's a little paranoid," Bernstein told him. "Ludwig has a complex. He thinks every little old winemaker is the Gestapo. When he sees one of 'them,' he tips me off."

Levy rolled his eyes, helplessly. "Jesus, just what we need."

That night, all the men and their wives went out to dinner again, and early in the evening, Davidson took Levy aside and said he'd spoken with "the governor."

"He'll take eight million dollars' worth to start with. Then he wants as much as you've got in smaller increments, every sixty or ninety days or so. He says twenty cents on the dollar is fine, just so long as you take care of the Baron and all these other guys out of that."

Levy said they had already agreed on how they would split the proceeds of any deal. At twenty cents on the dollar, for $8 million worth, they would be getting $1.6 million. He and Bernstein would split that fifty-fifty—$800,000 each. Bernstein, Hellmer and Keith Simpson—their American contact—would get $200,000 apiece out of their $800,-000 share. That left $200,000 to be divided among the Baron and John Davidson (with Davidson also getting paid directly by "the governor"). Levy would split his $800,-000 share—presumably equally—with Steve Berg and Gerald Kassap.

"The minute he said a million-six, my mind was working overtime," Levy says. "When I'd tell Steve and Kassap about it, I'd just forget the million part and tell them we'd gotten six hundred thousand dollars—three hundred thousand for Leonard and his boys, three hundred thousand for the three of us. Then I'd give them one hundred thousand each, and I'd have six hundred thousand dollars for myself. If that fuckin' deal with Mr. Todd ever came through, I'd have another five hundred fifty thousand dollars. That meant better than a million bucks for me."

Levy was ecstatic. After four months of running around in circles, he was finally about to make his first big score. He would leave for the United States in the next few days, he said, and he would let Davidson know how soon he could return with the stock. They would rendezvous in Dusseldorf within a week.

Their business concluded, Levy and Davidson returned to the dinner table. The restaurant was the finest in Dusseldorf, and everyone dined sumptuously. Davidson picked up the tab, peeling off twenty-pound notes like dollar bills. That made Levy feel even better. He's never happier than when he's living well—good food, good wine, nice clothes, a fancy car, a fine cigar, a beautiful woman; when someone else is paying for it—and Levy has a big score in the offing, too—well, as he says, "Forget about it; I'm in heaven."

The next afternoon, Levy, Bernstein and Hellmer had lunch together. Levy was beginning to trust Hellmer now, but he still felt a little nervous around him. "All the nudging, nodding and note-taking, and now he had a new little trick—he said we should use hand signals whenever we talked about certain things in a public place. We shouldn't say 'police' or 'FBI' or 'Gestapo' or whatever. And he showed us these *cockamamy* signals. Anytime we wanted to talk about the cops or the FBI, he said we should put our right index finger alongside our eye and pull down. Anytime we wanted to talk about the possibility of jail or getting arrested, we were supposed to put two fingers of our right hand around our left wrist, like bracelets. For some other thing, we were supposed to hold our nose or brush our ears or something. If I hadn't already made the deal for a million-six, I would have thought we were all crazy. I mean, watching him go through those signals was like watching some epileptic third-base coach giving signals to a batter. Hit. Bunt. Squeeze. Steal. Take two and hit to right. This guy was a ding-a-ling. And all the time he's signaling, he's also taking notes and nudging Leonard and nodding at winemakers. What a group of sophisticates we were."

After lunch, Levy called Steve Berg in Los Angeles to bring him up to date, and tell him to call Kassap. "I've only got about a million dollars' worth of merchandise left at my place," Levy told him. "Have Kassap get another eight million or so ready for me." Berg said he would call Kassap right away, and Levy agreed to call back. When he did, Berg told him Kassap was in New York.

"Look," Levy said, "this is important. We each stand to make one hundred thousand dollars on this deal. You try to get a hold of him back there. Me and Frannie are leaving Dusseldorf in the morning. I promised to show her Paris while we're here. I tried to get hotel reservations there, but they got some kind of *farkokte* air show going on, and everything's booked up. We'll have to play it by ear. I'll call you when I get settled."

But they never got settled. It was hot and smoggy and crowded when they landed at Orly Airport, and they took a cab to a half-dozen different hotels, all of which were fully booked.

Reluctantly, Levy told his wife, "I guess we'll just have to fly on to London."

First, though, he went to a pay phone in a post office to call Steve Berg. Kassap had returned home, and Berg set up a three-way conference call. Kassap said he'd sent most of the prepared stock to New York "on another deal." Levy exploded. "You did what? Listen, you jackass, I got a chance to make us all a fortune here, and *you're* sending *my* stock to New York." Kassap assured him he could get the stock back by the time Levy returned to Los Angeles. "Okay," Levy said, "today's Wednesday. I'll be in London tomorrow and in L.A. Friday or Saturday. You make sure you have that stock. I promised it to these guys, and if we back out, we're all dead men." He hung up and called Bernstein in Dusseldorf. He had planned to call Bernstein anyway to let him know when he'd be leaving Europe and to ask for help in financing the return trip. Now he debated telling him about the missing stock, too. On second thought, he decided not to say a word about it. Bernstein gave him a telephone number in Beverly Hills, and said he should call there when he got home. "They'll have one thousand dollars for you to get back here on," he said.

His business concluded for the day, Levy offered to show his wife a little of Paris—the Eiffel Tower, the *Arc de Triomphe*, the *Champs-Elysées*, the *Louvre*. He had been to Paris before, on dress-buying expeditions, but she had never seen the city before, and they spent a delightful afternoon wandering around like a couple of typical American tourists. Near sunset, they stopped to rest in one of those small parks that help make Paris so beautiful. After a few minutes, Frannie started to cry. Maybe it was the time of day, maybe it was the heat and the crowds, maybe it was the disappointment of having to see so much in so short a time. Whatever the cause, Frannie was upset—and angry. Levy had promised to show her Paris, she complained, and now they wouldn't even be staying overnight. What kind of vacation was that? Levy tried to explain that he had done everything he could to find hotel space, but there just weren't any rooms available. In the middle of their argument, a nicely dressed woman came over, carrying a small can with a slot in the top.

"*Pardon,*" she said, thrusting the can gently toward Levy.

Levy, assuming she was soliciting contributions for some French charity, shook his head and said he didn't want to make a donation. But she didn't seem to understand English, and she pushed the can closer to him.

"G'wan," he snapped, "scram, get outta here. I'm not giving you any money."

Other people in the park began to look at him, and both he and Frannie were getting embarrassed. But he was determined not to give in to the woman's entreaties.

Finally, the woman left. Five minutes later, she was back —with a *gendarme.*

"*Pardon, monsieur—*"

Levy didn't let him finish. "Don't '*Pardon monsieur*' me. I know French laws are a little different than American laws, but there's no way you're gonna convince me it's against the law not to contribute to some charity. I don't care if this broad's deaf, dumb and blind. I ain't giving her no money."

The *gendarme*, who stood remarkably silent during Levy's tirade, began again. *"Pardon, monsieur."* This time he finished his explanation. It seems that it cost one franc to sit on a bench in this park—the funds to be used for the maintenance of the park—and the woman with the can was merely collecting the fee. Sheepishly, Levy paid her and hustled his wife out of the park, amid the good-natured laughter of those around them who had witnessed the entire scene.

The Levys flew to London that evening, and went straight to a hotel reservation service, dead-tired from all their sightseeing—and arguing—in Paris. But the man in front of Levy in the reservation line was a Pakistani with very specific requirements for his room. It must not cost over six pounds and it must be brightly lit and have two bathtubs and a dressing area and—

"Twenty minutes it took him to get a room," Levy says. "When my turn came, I just said, 'Give me anything with a tub and a toilet and I'll be happy.'" He looked at Frannie. Outside of a few good meals in Dusseldorf, it really hadn't been much of a vacation for her. She was wan and drawn and still disappointed at having left Paris so quickly.

What the hell, Levy figured, I'll splurge. He told the woman behind the reservation desk to find him "a nice suite. I don't care what it costs."

That night, Alan and Frannie ate a quiet dinner in their $75 suite, in a fine hotel just off Hyde Park. Before going to bed, Levy telephoned Mario Denard to tell him he was back and wanted to talk to him in the morning about the Tom Wilson stock. They arranged to have breakfast in the hotel.

"When Mario shows up the next morning, he's carrying a briefcase. The minute we sit down in this restaurant, he puts it on the table, opens it up and takes the stock out. I *plotzed*. 'Not here, not here,' I'm whispering. A picture of Ludwig Hellmer and all his *farkokte* signs flashes through my mind. I start tugging on my right eye and tapping my wrists. Mario must've thought I'd gone bananas. I figured that with all the guys we had in this deal by now, Scotland Yard must be hot on our trail, and we sure as hell don't want to start waving our stock around the goddamn dining room like dinner napkins."

Levy suggested putting the stock in a safe deposit box until he returned from Los Angeles, but Denard said he had a better idea. "I think I may have a deal for us." Levy said that was fine with him. "You make the deal, and we'll split fifty-fifty. Just make sure I get at least fifty thousand dollars." Denard said he was sure he could do better than that—"for both of us."

Denard also cautioned Levy not to be too certain about his deal with John Davidson and "the governor." "They aren't the most reliable men in the world," he said. But Levy, skeptical from the outset, had finally been convinced by Davidson's smoothness that last night in Dusseldorf, and he muttered under his breath that he was a lot more worried about Denard than he was about Davidson. Aloud, he just told Denard he would contact him when he returned to Europe. "I'm hoping I can fly directly from L.A. to Dusseldorf. Then I'll stop back by here on my way back home. See if you can wrap your deal up by then."

Denard nodded. "Should be easy."

Chapter 5

As soon as he returned to Los Angeles, Levy picked up his little girl at his mother-in-law's house. He couldn't wait to get her home. She was only about fourteen months old then, but he took great delight in playing with her and talking to her and watching television with her. He treated her, alternately, as if she were a cuddly little kitten and a mature adult. At times, he all but ignored his wife, so single-minded was his attention to Nicole. This was such an occasion, but in time, he realized he had better get back to business. He left Frannie and Nicole in the living room and walked across the street to the tennis club to call Steve Berg.

"Kassap got that stock back yet?"

"No. Not exactly."

"Whaddya mean 'not exactly'? Does he have it or doesn't he?"

"Well, it was due back today air freight, but it hasn't been delivered yet. It should be here tomorrow at the latest."

Levy decided to call Fats Jackson and his doctor friend to make sure the San Fernando Valley bank loan had gone through as scheduled. The $20,000 he was going to get from that deal—actually $15,000 after Fats got his cut—would come in handy in Europe. He called the doctor first. No answer. He tried the doctor's exchange. The answering service said he was unavailable. Levy called Fats.

"As far as I know, he made the loan," Jackson said.

"Great. Did you get our twenty thousand dollars?"

"Well, no, but I think he's got all the money. We just have to pick it up."

Levy kept calling the doctor every thirty minutes. Finally, shortly before midnight, he got him. Dispensing with formalities the minute he heard the doctor's voice, he said, "Okay, doc, where's my money?"

"I can't talk now," the doctor replied.

"Well, you better—"

"Don't worry. Everything's okay. Call me tomorrow night at nine o'clock."

"Okay, but you better have my money. I'm going back to Europe in a couple of days."

Levy decided to make a few other calls. He checked on the Phoenix negotiations, the Hume Cannery loan and the transaction Mr. Todd was supposed to have long since completed in Switzerland. Nothing. Absolutely nothing.

"Everyone I called gave me one of these," he says, jerking his right fist up and down in front of his crotch. "No one knew where anyone was, but everyone was sure things were going smoothly and we'd have the money in no time at all. Wonderful. I had all this money out there and nothing but shit in my pocket. I was like a business with a million bucks in accounts receivable and two nickels in the cash register. But there wasn't much I could do. I'd done all the yelling and threatening I could. What the hell was I gonna do—call the cops and say, 'Hey, these guys are screwing me'?"

The next morning, Saturday, Levy walked over to the tennis club and called the number Bernstein had given him to get his $1,000. A man answered and told him to come over. The address was on Sunset Boulevard in Beverly Hills, an impressive-looking law office, but the man looked more like a Central American guerrilla than a Beverly

Hills lawyer—short, wiry, with jet-black hair and a heavy beard. He gave Levy the $1,000, and asked him to sign a receipt for it.

"Now, I was really feeling good," Levy recalls. "I hadn't been sure I would get the thousand dollars. I thought Leonard might be bullshitting me. But I got it so easy, with a bip and a bop and a boop. Next stop—a million-six."

From the attorney's office, Levy drove to Steve Berg's house. "Let's get going," he said. "Call Kassap and find out if he's got the stock back yet. I gotta call those guys in Dusseldorf today, and let them know when to expect me, so they can have our money waiting for us. This isn't a penny-ante game, you know. It's not like walking into the Bank of America on the corner to cash a ten-dollar check. They have to make arrangements in advance for six hundred thousand dollars." (Levy, of course, was still telling Berg and Kassap there was only $600,000 involved, not $1.6 million).

When Berg called Kassap, Kassap said he'd just checked with the airport, and the package had arrived, but there was no scheduled delivery in his area until Monday. Levy jerked the phone from Berg's hand. "Call 'em back and tell 'em we'll pick it up ourselves—right now!"

Levy and Berg drove to Kassap's plant, picked him up and drove all the way across town, about twenty-five miles, to the air freight terminal at the Los Angeles airport. But the man in charge of the terminal didn't know about Kassap's package. "It's big," Kassap told him, "I don't see how you could miss it." The man sorted through his bills and receipts: "Nope. Not here."

For the next hour, all of them—the man, an assistant, Levy, Berg and Kassap—pored through paperwork and packages, without success.

"Look," the man finally suggested, "why don't you guys go home. We'll keep looking, and as soon as we find it, I'll call you."

On the ride home, Levy ripped into Kassap. "Okay, you

son-of-a-bitch, something stinks here and you know it. Don't jerk me off any more, damn it! This is too big a deal for that. Where's the fucking stock?"

Berg tried to cool Levy off, but Levy just got madder. In time, he wore Kassap down, and Kassap admitted he still had all the stock in his garage; he'd never sent it to New York. Levy, he said, had spread his stock all over the whole goddamn world in a dozen different deals, and all Kassap had to show for it was that one lousy $5,000 check. They were supposed to be millionaires, he said, but he was stuck in East Los Angeles, sweating over his plant, while Levy was off galavanting around Paris and London and Dusseldorf with his wife. He wasn't sure he wanted to do business with Levy any more.

Levy was even more exasperated than Kassap by the futility of their ventures thus far, but he wasn't in the mood for commiseration. "Look, asshole, until I got involved, you didn't know what the fuck to do with this stock. Now we got a chance to get rich, you hear me? You're gonna get a hundred grand out of this. A hundred grand. You ever see that much dough before in your life? See it? Shit, you probably never even knew it existed. Now let's get that stock."

The three men drove the rest of the way to Kassap's house in silence. They loaded Berg's car with the stock, and took it back to Kassap's plant to sort through it. Levy wanted to take all the numbered stock back to Europe with him. He'd take his stamps and pens along with him, and prepare the stock there. He had no idea what the law was, but his instinct told him he'd probably have less trouble if he were arrested going through Customs with unprepared stock than with prepared stock. He also wanted to take along some of the numbered stock, though—the rawest of the unprepared stock, certificates without even a sequential number. Maybe he could find a European printer who would help him number those. He made a new inventory, and when he was through, he called Dusseldorf, and told Leonard Bernstein he expected to be back the first part of the week. "Call John Davidson, and have him and the governor meet us." Then he thought of a potential problem. "The merchandise fills one huge suitcase. How am I going to get that through German Customs?" Bernstein told him not to worry. He and the Baron would have everything arranged.

When Berg dropped Levy and the stock off in Cheviot Hills, Levy remembered he was supposed to call the doctor. He walked to the tennis club. The doctor was very vague over the phone. Levy started to threaten him. "You don't know who you're messin' with, doc. I ain't in this alone, you know—not a deal this big. My friends aren't the kind of guys you want to stiff. They'd as soon suck your eyeballs out as look at you. Now where's my money? You better have a good answer 'cause if you don't, I'm coming after you right now."

The doctor was silent for a moment. Then, very softly and deliberately, he said, "You can come over and get it this evening."

"That's more like it," Levy rasped. "You—"

"The FBI is here, too."

Levy stopped dead, suddenly deflated. "The who is where?"

"You heard me. The FBI is here. At my house. Now. Are you coming over or not?"

Levy decided, belatedly, to play it cool. "Look, doc, I don't know nothing about the FBI. All I know is you and I got a legitimate business deal, and you owe me and my partner twenty thousand dollars."

The doctor told Levy, "The FBI has your stock, and you're not getting any money. You want the stock back? Ask them for it."

"I ain't asking them for nothing. I don't even know what you're talking about with your FBI and your stock. All I know is you owe me twenty thousand dollars, and I'm going to get it." He hung up.

At first, Levy was inclined to believe the doctor. That's why he had turned coy and feigned ignorance of the stock —unconvincing though his performance probably was. But the more he thought about it, the more certain he was that he'd just been stiffed: "FBI my ass. The doctor just took me for a ride. He had the stock and the money and I was left with a handful of shit—again."

Levy didn't have time to pout over his latest blunder. He had to make reservations for his return to Europe the next day.

"I'd have the stock with me, so I wanted to go through just the one Customs, in Germany, where the Baron was supposed to set things up. I didn't want any part of Customs in any other country on the way."

He booked a TWA flight to New York, connecting with a Lufthansa flight to Glasgow and on to Dusseldorf, without changing planes. He checked all his luggage through to Dusseldorf, including the suitcase full of stock, and he stripped the suitcase of all identifying marks and labels. All he had was a baggage claim check, and if things got hot, he figured he could always throw that away—"or eat it"— and pretend he'd never seen the suitcase before in his life.

When he landed in New York, he called his mother in Miami. "I'm on my way to Europe, Mom. I'm gonna make a million dollars. You'll never have to work again your whole life."

She asked for details, but he begged off. "Don't worry," he told her. "I'll fill you in when everything's settled."

She wanted to talk longer, and he finally had to cut her short by telling her he might miss his flight if he didn't hang up. By the time they said goodbye, he almost *had* missed the flight. He raced to the boarding gate just in time.

"For some reason, the plane was about seventy-five percent full of Russian peasants and other East European immigrants," he recalls. "It was a small plane, a DC-1 or something—the Bucharest Special. They were mostly big, heavy women in black dresses with black bandanas and babushkas around their heads. I felt like I was in a concentration camp somewhere with no one to talk to. I couldn't even sleep. They just kept jabbering away in Russian or Rumanian or whatever, and about three o'clock in the morning, they opened these brown paper bags and took out this vile, smelly stuff for lunch. It was like being on a cross-country bus in the worst part of Mexico. The whole goddamn place smelled like a Polish delicatessen. If I hadn't felt so good about all the money I had waiting for me in Dusseldorf, I would've spent the whole flight puking my guts out."

The entire flight from Los Angeles to New York to Glasgow to Dusseldorf—including layovers in New York and Glasgow—took more than eighteen hours, and by the time he landed in Dusseldorf, Levy was utterly exhausted. His first thought, when he saw the baggage being unloaded and driven to the terminal on an open cart was, "Thank God it ain't raining. I got about ten million dollars' worth of stock in a porous cloth bag; one big drizzle, and the stuff is ruined."

It didn't rain, though, and as he approached the Customs area, he saw Bernstein and the Baron. Bernstein was carrying a camera and a light meter, which thoroughly baffled Levy. "How the hell's that gonna help us sneak through Customs?" he wondered. "Or is he just going to capture our arrest on film for posterity?" Levy looked toward them for an answer, but they pretended not to notice him. He shrugged and carried his bags toward Customs, figuring the Baron might not have been able to set anything up after all. "Maybe I can squeeze through the crowd, quiet-like, and no one will see me," he thought, without much hope. Then, just as the Customs agent was getting ready to examine his bags, Bernstein burst from the crowd, camera clicking and flashbulbs flashing. "You're the one," he shouted at the Customs agent, "You're the one, you're the one we want."

Before the stunned Customs agent could regain his equanimity, Bernstein was on top of him, overwhelming him. "I'm with an American motion picture studio. I'm a producer. You're perfect for our next film. We've been looking all over Europe for a fresh, new face for a very important role. You haven't been in the movies before, have you?"

Levy blanched. "Jesus Christ," he thought, "those idiots can't really expect to get away with a bullshit ruse like that, can they? These Customs guards must see slicker numbers than this in their sleep."

But Bernstein was virtually smothering the Customs agent, and the agent was responding to his directions— "Let me see your profile. Now the left one. Oh, good, good, perfect. Now full-face." Levy just shook his head: "Good thing the guy doesn't look too bright. With his belly and his pistola, he looks like a poor man's Wyatt Earp." The guard had a two-way radio in his right hand, and as he whirled and pranced about in response to Bernstein's increasingly authoritative commands, he almost poked several travelers in the eye with the radio aerial. The scene had begun to take on the look of low comedy—if not outright camp— when the Baron, biding his time perfectly, came running up and threw his arms around Levy. "Mon ami, mon ami," he gushed, showering Levy with kisses. "C'est bien de tu voir encore. Nous serons riches."

With that, he picked up the suitcase filled with stock, gestured for Levy to pick up the one with his clothes in it and—jabbering all the way—escorted Levy past Customs, through the terminal and out to a waiting car. They were still laughing over the success of their amateurish little trick when Bernstein joined them a few minutes later. Then they drove, still giggling like high-school pranksters, to the Intercontinental Hotel.

Levy checked in—Bernstein had previously made the reservation—and they went immediately to his room to examine the stock.

"Leonard damn near had an orgasm when I opened that suitcase," Levy says. "I don't care who you are, ten million dollars' worth of stock is a pretty sight to see. We all joined hands and danced a little jig and sang. We were gonna be rich. Rich!"

Bernstein called John Davidson, and arranged a meeting for two o'clock that afternoon in the Esplanade Hotel, where Bernstein was staying. The governor would be there, too, Davidson said. He was flying in from London. They could eat a leisurely lunch together, drink a toast to their mutual enrichment and then adjourn to Bernstein's room to complete their transaction. Levy would have his money in a matter of days.

When Bernstein hung up, the Baron let out a whoop of joy, and the men began dancing anew.

At the appointed time, Levy and Bernstein drove the Baron to his apartment, then drove on to the Esplanade. They took the suitcase full of stock up to Bernstein's room and left it there. Then they walked into the hotel cocktail lounge, where they saw Ludwig Hellmer. He was also waiting, he said, for Davidson and the governor. Everyone ordered drinks—beer for Hellmer, Campari and soda for the others. "Right away, Ludwig starts in with his note-taking again," Levy says. "But this time, I didn't care. I mean, we were going to be millionaires by dinnertime. Notes, shmotes. Who gives a shit?"

When two o'clock came and went with no sign of Davidson, Levy began to get a little uneasy. At two-thirty, still no Davidson. Finally, at two-forty-five, he walked in—alone.

Before he could even say hello, Levy pounced on him. "Where's the governor?"

"I don't know. I thought he'd be here with you."

"What—"

"He changed his mind about flying, and decided to take the ferry over and drive instead."

"Well, why don't you call London. Maybe he hasn't left yet. I didn't come seven thousand miles to sit in a bar all day. I can do that at home."

Davidson excused himself and called London. When he returned, he said he'd spoken to "an associate of the governor's. He will try to locate the governor, and call us back within the hour."

Fifty minutes later, the hotel paged Davidson. Again he excused himself. He was all smiles when he returned. "I have just spoken to the governor. He had to go to Luxembourg suddenly to transact some very important business at his bank. He wants us to meet him there. That's better for you anyway. That's where his money is, and you can get your money right away. He expects to be available in Luxembourg within the next forty-eight hours or so."

Levy wasn't very happy about that. "I sure as hell didn't want to carry that stock across another border. I thought that was taking too many chances. Luxembourg, in particular, I didn't want to go to. That's the headquarters for the European Coal and Steel Community, and the Common Market has some big offices there, too. They gotta have pretty good security there. Probably an Interpol office. Maybe an FBI listening post and some CIA types there, too, for all I knew. It's a pretty rich country, one of the richest, per capita, in the world. Rich people usually like to have a good police force to keep them rich. Smart cops and Interpol and Freddie, Bernie and Irving I can do without." But Levy didn't have much choice in the matter. "Okay," he told Davidson. "You find out what hotel he'll be at, and we'll contact him there."

When the meeting broke up, Levy, Bernstein and Hellmer drove back to the Baron's apartment. He greeted them with champagne, but quickly put the bottles away when he saw they were in no mood for celebrating. Their general crankiness only made the language barrier that much more frustrating. Tempers were short, angry words were exchanged and the Baron suggested calling in another friend to act as translator. She had worked with him before, he explained, and she was a shrewd businesswoman. She spoke English, French and Italian fluently, but she could do more than just translate for them. If the governor made any last-minute attempts to slicker them out of their money, she would see through him. The woman lived in Brussels, the Baron said. He would call her immediately. She could be in Dusseldorf that evening.

In the course of their afternoon discussion, the men agreed on one other point: When Davidson came by that evening to confirm the details of the Luxembourg meeting, they would demand that he disclose the governor's identity. "I'm through dealing with some *farkokte* phantom," Levy said. "This guy's gonna take eight million dollars' worth of stock off our hands. He must have a name. I want it."

After dinner, the woman from Brussels—she was introduced simply as Linda—came to the Baron's house. Levy and Bernstein liked her immediately. "She was very attractive, very European, very sophisticated," Levy says, "a Zsa Zsa Gabor with brains."

As Linda and the Baron spoke, the Baron mentioned rather casually that he had made a great deal of money from his sale of the Elmyr de Hory art forgeries. But the money was in a Swiss bank, and because he was a wanted man in Switzerland, he couldn't go after it. He had a lawyer in Switzerland, but the lawyer wanted more money. Levy asked Linda to translate their conversation. When she did, Levy volunteered to help the Baron. "As soon as we get our dough from the governor, we'll work it out," he assured her. She translated his encouragement for the Baron.

The Baron was overjoyed, and when Davidson arrived, he found everyone in better spirits. "Everything is taken care of," he assured them.

But Levy wasn't quite as exuberant as the others. "There's

one thing we still haven't taken care of," he told Davidson.
"Just who the hell is this governor of yours?"

"I've already told you I'm not at liberty to say just yet.
You will all learn that in due time."

"Now is due time. Right now."

With that, Levy started to get nasty. Linda tried to restrain him: "We're all partners, Alan." The Baron took
Linda aside, and explained that he felt a certain respon-
sibility for Davidson's performance. It was the Baron who
had brought Davidson into the deal, and if Davidson didn't
cooperate, the Baron would have to take care of him. During the final words of their whispered conversation, the
Baron raised his voice just enough for Davidson and the
others to hear him. The malevolence in his tone was un-
mistakable. Davidson decided to cooperate.

The governor, he said, was Ernest Shinwell, a graduate
of Harrow, the same school that Winston Churchill and
Sir Robert Peel had attended. Shinwell's father was a member of the House of Lords and a confidante of the Queen.
He had served in Prime Minister Clement Attlee's postwar
cabinet. The governor, clearly, was a member of one of the
most prominent and influential families in all of England.
That, Davidson said, should set their minds at ease: "An
English gentleman does not deceive his business associates."

Thus mollified, Levy and his friends began making plans
for the trip to Luxembourg. At first, they decided to fly.
But the Baron, speaking through Linda, said there was a
greater likelihood of difficulty with Customs if they flew
than if they drove. "Okay," Levy said, "Let's drive." One
car, they agreed, was all they should take; "no sense looking like a football caravan or funeral procession." Davidson
volunteered to drive. "Just what we need," Levy said. "We're
gonna try to sneak across the border, and you want to do it
in the only royal-blue Cadillac convertible on the whole
continent."

But everyone wanted to go along, and Davidson's car
was the only one big enough to carry them all in relative

comfort. Davidson and Levy would be going, of course. So would Bernstein, Hellmer and the Baron. Linda would meet them later. It was agreed. Levy would spend the next two nights with the Baron, and the others would return to their hotels. They would rendezvous the morning after next for the drive to Luxembourg.

When everyone left, the Baron asked Linda to stay behind. He had something he wanted to talk to Levy about, and he would need her help in translation. Levy waited. "While you were back in the United States," the Baron said, "I talked to a couple of men who may want to buy some stock. One is in Italy. He has his own bank. But he's embezzled a lot of money, and he figures he can use the stock to cover himself."

Levy said he wasn't interested. "We got enough deals going without getting involved with some bank embezzler. How's he gonna get the money to buy the stock from us? Embezzle some more from his bank? Forget it."

The Baron said he had another friend whose position might make a deal more attractive. "He's with one of the Latin American embassies here, and he's lost a lot of money gambling. He needs some money in a hurry, but he doesn't have any collateral for a loan. I thought about your stock. If we could get him one hundred thousand dollars' worth, he would give us all passports and papers that would identify us as citizens of his country."

As the Baron spoke, Levy—whose mind was already in the governor's bank vault in Luxembourg—found himself waiting for the other shoe to drop: What was the Baron's friend willing to pay for the stock? And what the hell did Levy need with a Latin American passport? When no explanation was forthcoming, Levy asked the Baron just those questions.

"He can't pay us anything," the Baron said. "He doesn't have any money. That's why he needs the stock. We could use the papers to travel around incognito."

If Levy hadn't grown so fond of the Baron, he probably

would have laughed in his face. Even so, he was somewhat less than gentle in his response:

"Look, what do I want with a banana republic passport? Travel around? Travel around as what? A banana? I can't speak Spanish except for *manana, gringo* and Tijuana. Who am I going to be—Jose Gonzales from hotsy-totsy *Espana* cockalotta? Somebody's gonna come up to me and say something in Spanish, and I'm gonna answer, 'Yeah and a lot of tortillas and enchiladas to you, too.' Come on, Baron, I—" Suddenly, an idea hit him.

"Say, could this friend of yours get us a license to open a gambling casino in his country? That might be worth the hundred grand and then some. Owning a casino in a place like that is like having a license to steal. You tell him to get us a promise from the government, in writing, and maybe we'll talk about a deal."

Before Linda could finish translating, Levy started having second thoughts. "To tell you the truth, I wouldn't believe anything any Latin American government told me, in writing or not. They're all about as stable and honest as a Tijuana whorehouse. By the time we give him the stock and he makes his loan, his whole government could be overthrown. I'd be left holding my *putz,* saying, 'He went that-away.' "

But the Baron insisted they should at least talk to his friend. Levy, he said, had access to $800 million worth of stock. So far, he'd used only a fraction of it. What was a piddling $100,000? If there was any chance of their making something on the Latin American deal, why not give it a try. At worst, they'd lost the $100,000 worth of stock. Big deal.

That made sense to Levy, so the next day, they invited the ambassador out for a drink. He spoke only Spanish and French, and the Baron tried to translate. Sure, the ambassador said, opening a casino would be no problem at all. In fact, they could probably open a hotel, too, if they wanted.

And a few stores. And a bank. The Baron translated, haltingly but straight-faced. Levy exploded. "A bank we're gonna open? Come on, this guy is full of shit. It's all shit. He probably isn't even an ambassador—just some tourist who blew his wad at the tables and thinks he can play us for suckers to bail himself out. I'm not giving him a quarter."

But the Baron was reluctant to be rude to his friend.

"Tell him we have to leave the country," Levy suggested. "Tell him we'll call him again when we return." Under his breath, he added, "Don't call us, we'll call you. Yeah, in a pig's ass we will."

That night, Levy and the Baron invited Bernstein over to map their final plans. Before they could begin, the Baron had yet another scheme. Levy tried to dissuade him from discussing it, but the Baron was insistent. He had several friends, he said, who had original oil paintings—"very valuable"—so valuable, in fact, that they were among the world's best-known paintings. They had been stolen from various museums and art galleries and replaced with forgeries. That was the beauty of it, the Baron said; no one ever knew they were missing. Levy could buy a half-million-dollar picture for $200,000 worth of stock, maybe less. Wasn't that a great buy?

No, Levy said, that most certainly was not a great buy. "What the hell am I going to do with an original Chagall that no one knows is an original and I can't admit is an original? I can't sell it, right? If I sell it as a copy, I don't get any money. If I sell it as an original, I go to jail. So what do I do—hang it over my toilet and invite my art-lover neighbor over for a drink and say, 'Oh, by the way, wouldn't you like to go take a leak, and be sure and notice my original Chagall while you're at it'? With my luck, he'll piss all over the goddamn painting. Or he won't know Chagall from O. J. Simpson. Or maybe he really will know, and he'll tell me I'm either a liar or a fool since everyone knows that the original is hanging in the *Louvre*."

The Baron, taken aback by the ferocity of Levy's attack, sat sulking silently for a few minutes before Bernstein chimed in. "Look, Alan, the pictures may help us yet." Levy jumped from his seat. "You, too? You both nuts?" Bernstein asked him to "Listen to me before you start calling everyone nuts."

"I've opened a bank account in Switzerland for us to put our money into when we close the deal with Shinwell. We gotta have a cover story, though. I mean where did we all of a sudden get a million-six, right? Well, while you were back in the States, me and the Baron put together a little portfolio." He produced a black, loose-leaf notebook, and began flipping through it. There were several photographs inside, each showing a painting—works by Goya and Chagall and Rembrandt and Van Gogh, among others. Attached to the back of each photo was a letter attesting to the authenticity of that particular painting. The letters were signed by art critics and curators.

"Some of these paintings are the ones the Baron told you about," Bernstein said, "and some of them are forgeries. It doesn't matter. I'll call my banker in Basel before we leave in the morning, and tell him I'm about to complete a large transaction. I'll say I'm selling several priceless pieces of art from my personal collection, and he should be ready to accept and process a very large cash deposit. When we get there, I'll even show him this portfolio. You know, *shmaltz* it up a little for him—lay it on thick."

Levy liked the sound of that. "Good, we're covered on both ends. I can hardly wait till morning."

That night, there was another big dinner party. "All the co-co-co-conspirators were there," Levy says. "We ate and drank wine till two in the morning. John Davidson picked up the check again, and every time I started to act a little skeptical or ask any questions, he'd say, 'Don't

worry.' That was his national anthem, for Christ's sake.
Not 'God Save the Queen,' but 'Don't worry.' No matter
what happened, no matter what you said, John was always ready with his 'Don't worry.' He reminded me of this
fighter I once managed in San Diego. He'd be getting his
brains beat out, and he'd keep telling you, 'Don't worry.
I got him.' "

Until Levy had gotten involved in the stock swindle,
managing the fighter had been just about the most frustrating experience of his life. The fighter's name was Clifford Gray, and Levy—selecting his opponents carefully—had
brought him along slowly and had him tentatively set for
a bout with then-ranking heavyweight Alejandro Lavorante
of Argentina. All Gray had to do to get the fight—and a
big pay-day—was not get himself killed (or humiliated)
in a non-title bout with world light-heavyweight champion Archie Moore. Moore had helped train Gray, and
Levy thought he would be willing to carry his old sparring
buddy for eight or ten rounds before knocking him out—
especially since Moore had a title fight with Giulio Rinaldi
of Italy coming up himself in a month and he needed the
work.

"The fight was in Nogales," Levy says, "and for them,
it was a big deal. The whole town was plastered with bill-
boards welcoming 'Killer Gray,' and my dumb son-of-a-
bitch of a fighter believes it all. In the first round, he hits
Archie with a right cross. It didn't hurt Archie, but it
startled him. Then Clifford hits him another right cross.
This one Archie at least feels. He shuffles around until the
bell rings, and he walks to his corner scowling at Clifford
like Clifford's been a naughty boy and daddy just caught
him and if he isn't careful, daddy is gonna break all his
fingers and toes.

"I'm sitting in the third row ringside, and I get up and
go running into Clifford's corner. 'What are you,' I ask
him, 'an idiot? All you gotta do is walk around. Don't

take no chances. If he hits you, fall down. Don't go hitting him. He might get mad and really hurt you. You don't wanna blow the Lavorante fight, do you?' "

Gray looked up at Levy. "Alan, I think I got him."

Levy couldn't believe his ears. "You think you got who, Clifford?"

"Archie. I think I got him. I think I can take him."

"Clifford, are you listening to me? Clear the cobwebs, Clifford. He hasn't even *tried* to hit you yet. You've given him your two best shots, and all he did was stop smiling. You haven't got him, and if you're not careful, you're not gonna have nobody."

The second round was better. Gray boxed and backtracked and Moore pawed after him, apparently willing to treat the two first-round punches as forgivable overeagerness. Then, in the third round, Gray came out swinging. He backed Moore against the ropes and started pummeling him. Moore was a cagey old pro who knew how to protect himself, and none of the blows really hurt him. He caught most of them on his gloves and forearms. But the fans thought Gray was about to knock the champ out. They were on their feet, screaming. Levy saw what was happening. "Any second," he told himself, "Archie is gonna hit this guy in the mouth and he'll fall right through the floor."

Miraculously, it seemed, Moore made no attempt to fight back before the round ended. He just shook his head sadly at Gray and strolled to his corner. Gray bounded back to his stool, and Levy was there waiting for him, spluttering with righteous indignation. "You're looking to get killed, Clifford. You wanna get killed? What are you anyway, nuts? You wanna die so bad, go jump off a bridge. Don't let it happen right here where I have to watch. Please, Clifford. Just dance around. No, don't even dance. Shuffle. Let him hit you. He won't hurt you. I promise. Just don't get him mad."

Gray shook his head vigorously. "This is my round,

Alan. I got him. I'm going to knock him out. I'm going to knock out the world light-heavyweight champion."

Levy was pleading now. "Please, Clifford, for me. I've got so much invested in you. Please don't do this to me. Listen to me."

The bell rang for the fourth round, and Moore came out to meet Gray, seemingly no more concerned than he had been in the first three rounds. Suddenly, he hit Gray with a right hook. Gray sank to the canvas, then struggled to his feet. Moore hit him again. He went down again. And again. The third time, he didn't get up. The fight was over. Levy rushed to his fallen fighter. The trainer brought him around with smelling salts. Levy glanced balefully down at him: "How could you do this to us, Clifford?" Gray stared straight up at his manager, eyes unblinking: "Don't worry. I'll get him next round."

"That was John Davidson," Levy says. "Another Clifford Gray. Another 'Don't worry' guy. Just what I needed."

But Levy was beginning to trust John Davidson, his misgivings notwithstanding. He decided to give him the unnumbered stock to hold until they returned from Luxembourg. "I kept the eight million dollars' worth of numbered stock we were going to sell to Shinwell, but I didn't see any sense in carting the two million or so of unnumbered stock around, too. Me and Leonard would probably go see his banker in Switzerland after the meeting in Luxembourg. Why *shlep* the extra stock? When we were all through, I could come back to Dusseldorf and see about getting it numbered. By then, maybe Shinwell would be ready to buy some more."

Levy gave Davidson the unnumbered stock, and Davidson said he'd have his girl friend keep it for him. "It'll be safe with her," he said.

The next morning, still groggy from all the wine, Levy called Steve Berg in Los Angeles to tell him he was going to Luxembourg to pick up their money. Berg said he'd fly to Dusseldorf in a few days to pick up his share. After the call, Levy and Davidson piled into the front seat of Davidson's Cadillac for the drive to Luxembourg. Bernstein, Hellmer and the Baron rode in back. They made the drive in about five hours, taking their time and stopping to eat once on the way. Neither their luggage nor the car was searched crossing the border into Luxembourg. They just showed their passports and drove merrily on.

When they got to Luxembourg, Davidson drove to the Holiday Inn in the nation's capital—also named Luxembourg—where they'd be staying. But Levy was in no hurry to check in. "I didn't come to Luxembourg to sit in a Holiday Inn watching television. I can do that in Bakersfield or Queens. I wanna see Shinwell's bank."

Davidson said that was fine with him, and when they had driven alongside the bank, he pointed it out to Levy.

"You wouldn't think a grown man would fall in love with a building," Levy says, "but that's just what I did. Most of the European banks I'd seen were little second-story offices with a dirty shingle hanging out. But my bank —already I was thinking of Shinwell's bank as my bank— was a beautiful new building right on the corner. It was beautiful. Gorgeous. All chrome and silver on the outside. Big. A regular Bank of America headquarters, only prettier. And it was mine. My bank. There was a park next to it and City Hall nearby. I tell you, it was a wonderful sight. It was almost as good as having the money itself."

With Levy thus satisfied, Davidson drove back to the Holiday Inn. But the excitement of seeing Shinwell's bank wore off in about the time it took Levy to unpack, and he was soon hounding Davidson to see whether Shinwell had arrived yet. Davidson called Shinwell's hotel, and was told that he hadn't arrived yet, but was expected, "sometime this evening."

Levy wasn't satisfied. "He isn't here yet? I thought you said—"

"Don't worry," Davidson said. "He's coming. The hotel said so. Don't worry."

Bernstein agreed there was nothing to worry about. "Calm down, Alan. He'll be here. Let's relax and have a drink and go downstairs for dinner."

Dinner, Levy says, was "the worst meal I ever had in my life. Always before, John Davidson had taken us to good restaurants, but this was just awful, and I got more and more pissed as the night wore on."

Over coffee, Levy demanded that Davidson call Shinwell's hotel again. Davidson pleaded for more time: "At least let me finish dinner." But Levy didn't want to wait any more. He was growing more uneasy by the minute. The whole venture was beginning to feel like a wild-goose chase. Davidson would go make his call, Levy figured, and when he came back, he'd have "another bullshit story about how the governor got delayed in London and we should meet him in Warsaw, by way of Madrid, Vienna and Yokohama."

Levy was getting ready to pounce on Davidson, but when Davidson returned from the telephone, he said Shinwell had arrived and would see them at nine o'clock in his hotel.

Levy—by nature, a man of mercurial moods—shifted again from angry skepticism to anticipatory euphoria. "If the guy was gonna screw us, I figured he wouldn't show his face at all. Now that we were gonna go see him, I knew the money was just around the corner."

It was decided that Levy and Bernstein would accompany Davidson to Shinwell's hotel, and report back later to the others. The hotel was in the hills above the city and the Alzette River, and Davidson—driving slowly and making two wrong turns—took almost ninety minutes to complete the trip. When he pulled alongside the hotel, it was nine-forty-five. They were forty-five minutes late. But Davidson appeared unperturbed. He pointed out two cars

parked adjacent to the hotel. They were Rolls Royce convertibles, "Corniches, the most expensive and exclusive
model the company produces. Those are the governor's,"
he said with just a touch of arrogance. "Forty thousand dollars each."

Levy nodded, impressed.

The hotel impressed him, too. It was a traditional European hotel—old, well-finished, in a beautiful, tree-lined
setting that reminded him of the lakeside resorts he'd seen
on Lake Michigan as a boy. The lobby was old-fashioned,
with wicker-type furniture and muted colors, and as they
walked in, Davidson pointed to two couples sitting together on facing sofas.

"It was Shinwell, his wife, another man and his wife,"
Levy says. "One of the guys was about five-foot-ten or so,
very clean-cut, with sandy-brown hair. He looked like he
was in his early thirties, until you really examined him.
Then you could tell from the small wrinkles around his
eyes that he was probably about ten years older than that.
I was hoping he was Shinwell because the other guy
looked like he was standing in a hole—like maybe he'd
been married and divorced once before, and his first wife got
custody of his legs. He was maybe two inches taller than
Willie Shoemaker. Just my luck, that turns out to be Shinwell—a midget I need yet; I ain't got enough problems."

Shinwell was wearing plaid slacks and a Navy blue blazer
with gold buttons and a rosette in the lapel. The buttons,
he explained after they were introduced, had been "my
regiment's buttons." He had had his tailor cut them off his
military tunic and sew them on the blazer in place of con-
ventional buttons. The rosette, he said, was emblematic
of a medal he had been awarded during World War II—"the
Order of St. George."

He only mentioned the decorations, he said, because he
noticed that Levy also wore a rosette in his lapel—one
emblematic of the *croix de guerre*. Had Levy fought for

the French? he asked. Levy looked momentarily perplexed. The *croix de guerre*? He knew that some military heroes, especially those in Europe, often wore the small rosettes with their civilian dress clothes to show that they had significant medals at home, but he had certainly never won the *croix de guerre*—or any other medal. He took the rosette out of his lapel and looked at it. Suddenly, he remembered. He had bought the jacket at Eric Ross, an exclusive men's store in Beverly Hills, and the manager of the store had jokingly offered to throw the rosette in without charge, "so you can impress all your friends." Levy had accepted the offer and the manager had pinned the rosette in the lapel. Levy had just as quickly forgotten all about it. Now he put it back in the lapel.

"Yeah, the *croix de guerre*," he told Shinwell with a studied nonchalance. "Sure. Almost forgot. I was a big hero. Killed a lotta gooks in a Fifth Avenue haberdashery. Then I cut myself taking a leak on bivouac and got a Purple Heart. You too?"

Bernstein nudged Levy. Shinwell looked like exactly what Davidson had promised—suave, sophisticated, impeccably dressed, obviously a man of bearing and culture. He might not take kindly to Levy's barracks humor. "Cool it," Bernstein hissed to his partner.

After the formalities were complete, the two women excused themselves, and the five men sat down at a long, rectangular table in a small lounge just off the main hotel lobby. Shinwell and the other man sat on one side. Levy and Bernstein sat across from them. Davidson sat at the head of the table, a position befitting his role as middleman. The foot of the table was butted against the wall. As soon as everyone had settled into his seat, Shinwell said he would like to hear the entire story of the stock. Who, he inquired, would be the spokesman? "Me," Levy said, and he proceeded to relate—for what seemed like the tenthousandth time—the story of how he had gotten the stock and what he had been doing with it. Davidson, he figured, must have told Shinwell all this already, but maybe Shinwell wanted to hear it from the horse's mouth. Or maybe he just wanted time to size Levy up—or to compare what he said now with what he'd told Davidson earlier. Whatever, if he wanted to hear it again, Levy would oblige.

"I wasn't very comfortable talking to him though," Levy recalls. "It wasn't that he said or did anything wrong; I just had this feeling that he thought he was superior to the rest of us. The guy he'd brought with him didn't do anything to contradict that either. He really was fawning over Shinwell, really subservient. Shinwell had this aristocratic, autocratic bearing, and he seemed to sneer, rather than smile. When I finished talking about the stock, he just said, 'Well, yes, I may be interested.' I figured he was just maneuvering for bargaining position, so I decided to pile on a little bullshit. I told him all about my degree in advanced economics and Leonard's work as one of America's leading architects, and when that didn't seem to impress him too much, I decided to go all the way. 'This deal isn't all mine, you know,' I said. 'I represent some very powerful people in the United States. I don't think I have to tell you who I mean, except their last names have a little different sound than Levy and Bernstein. *Capice?*'"

Shinwell nodded wordlessly.

"Good," Levy said, "we understand each other. I just wanted you to know that my friends will be *very* unhappy if things don't work out quite right. Now, let me tell you a little about how you can use this stock."

When Levy started talking about collateralized loans and "padded" financial statements, Shinwell chuckled softly to himself.

"What's the matter?" Levy asked.

"Oh, nothing, nothing. But I do think, my good man, I may know a little more about this sort of thing than you do. After all, I do own my own bank."

Levy agreed that his course in elementary stock-swindling probably was a bit unnecessary under the circumstances, and Shinwell—his fingers steepled in front of his face—seemed pleased. He asked to examine the samples Levy had brought along. "Very good, very good," he murmured when he was through with them. He handed them back to Levy. "I'll need forty-eight hours to determine if I can use it," he said. "You give me all the stock now, and in forty-eight hours, I'll give it back to you or give you your money."

Levy was flabbergasted. "What do you mean you'll *see* if you can use it? What's this forty-eight hours crap? John Davidson said the deal was already set. He said you'd checked everything out, and we could collect our million-six right now. What do you need forty-eight hours for?"

Calmly, Shinwell explained how he had recently tried to dispose of some counterfeit IBM stock. "It was very poorly done," he said. "I was hurt rather badly in the transaction. I want to be sure that won't happen again. I'm going to be using your stock to make a seven-million-dollar loan, and I want to be careful."

Levy glared at Davidson, who managed to be looking out the window, into the dark night. "Why didn't you tell us he wasn't ready to deal?" Levy demanded. Davidson didn't answer. Levy turned back to Shinwell. "Okay, here's what I'll do. I'll stay in my hotel for forty-eight hours. You find out if you can use the stock, and you call me. But I'm not leaving the stock with you. When you're ready to pay for it, you get it—not before."

Shinwell insisted he had to have the stock first. "I want to show it to the right people, make sure we won't have any difficulty when we make the transaction itself. You don't have to worry about my running off with it."

The word "worry" acted like an alarm clock—or Pavlovian bell—on John Davidson. "That's right," he told Levy, "don't worry." Levy, stupefied that Davidson had the audacity to speak after having misled them so long, was speechless. Shinwell continued to argue for the stock. Finally, Levy agreed to think about it overnight. "I'll have to check with my associates in the United States, too," he told Shinwell.

Shinwell nodded, a nod of curt dismissal, it seemed to Levy. He started to object, then got up to leave. "Talk to you tomorrow."

Without shaking hands, he beckoned to Bernstein and Davidson and wheeled toward the door.

As soon as the three of them were in the car for the drive back to the city proper, Davidson rather cautiously asked Levy what he thought of Shinwell.

"He's a smooth, polished little pipsqueak," Levy replied. "He may be your governor, but he ain't mine. He ain't fooling me with that British accent and all those military decorations. What did he say one of those was—the Medal of St. George or some such shit? He won it at Dunkirk? Well, I got news for your governor. His boys were retreating at Dunkirk. Who wants that kind of medal?"

Davidson started to interrupt.

"I'm not through," Levy told him. "Governor or not, I don't care if he's the King of England. He better come up with my million-six, or he's gonna be sawed off a little more."

Davidson turned to Bernstein for support, but Bernstein lost little time in showing he, too, was no longer intimidated by Shinwell's impressive background. "Ernie baby's gonna have a lot of trouble on his hands if we don't get our dough," Bernstein said. Ernie baby. The very words left Davidson aghast.

"D-D-D-Don't worry," he stammered. "The governor is completely trustworthy. If you give him the stock, as he requests, I'd stake my life that he'd get it back to you—either that or the money."

A glimmer of malice lit Levy's eye. "I'm glad to hear you

say that, John," he said quietly, "because that's exactly what you would be staking—your life. If he screws me out of that stock, you're the first guy I'm coming after. If he goes bye-bye, so do you, John. You're a dead man."

Chapter 6

Back at their hotel, Levy gave Ludwig Hellmer and the Baron a brief summary of the meeting with Shinwell. Linda had driven over from Dusseldorf by then, and she, too, listened to the report. Levy was adamant about not relinquishing the stock until Shinwell paid for it. "I don't know how all of you feel," he said, "but I have no intention of giving his lordshit eight million dollars' worth of stock until he comes up with the money. I'll give him a few samples, but that's it." The Baron said he agreed. So did Bernstein and Hellmer and Linda.

The next morning, Shinwell called. He wouldn't need the forty-eight hours, he said. He'd decided he could use the stock. He would be over about eleven o'clock to take inventory, if that was okay, and all the details could be worked out then. Levy hung up, beaming. When he reported the conversation to his friends—all of whom had come up for breakfast—there was bedlam in the room. The Baron was hugging and kissing Levy. The others were jumping up and down on the bed. Even John Davidson shed his staid British exterior long enough to cackle, "See, I told you so, I told you so. I said you shouldn't worry."

At eleven sharp, a nattily-dressed Shinwell knocked on the door. Levy let him in and showed him where the stock was. Shinwell sorted through it all, and confirmed the $1.6 million price for $8 million worth of numbered stock. He also said he would like to buy the $2 million worth of unnumbered stock in thirty days. He would have to do some work on that, he said, so all he could offer was $250,-ooo. That was fine with Levy. Shinwell said he would probably want to buy additional $2-million increments, at the same price, every thirty days "for quite some time to come."

Levy struggled to keep his eyes from rolling to the ceiling. "We can probably work out something like that," he said, his voice fairly squeaking with excitement. "On this first million-six, where do we get the money?"

Shinwell suggested Levy bring the stock to his bank at ten o'clock the next morning. "I'll be waiting for you inside, and you can meet my banker." That idea didn't appeal to Levy. He remembered the near-disaster in Vancouver, and he didn't want to go through that again. Besides, on the off-chance that the law was after him, he didn't want to be caught in the bank with the stock. "I'll meet you outside the bank," he told Shinwell. "You can take it in and get the money. I'll wait out front for you." Shinwell said he had no objections to that arrangement.

"How do you plan to handle the money?" Shinwell asked.

Bernstein jumped into the conversation for the first time. He told Shinwell the name of his bank in Basel, and said they would probably drive there with the money. Shinwell looked skeptical, but said nothing.

The next morning, Levy and Bernstein left Hellmer, Linda and the Baron at the hotel and drove to the bank. They met Davidson in the park across the street, and he pointed out Shinwell's two Corniches parked out front. "The governor is inside. I will tell him you're here."

When Davidson returned, Levy and Bernstein were leaning on one of the Corniches. Haughtily, Davidson informed them, "The governor would not appreciate your elbows on his Corniche." Levy looked at Bernstein: "Who is this Charlie McCarthy telling us what to do with our elbows?" Davidson ignored the comment. "Do you have the stock?" he asked. Levy nodded. "Good," Davidson said. "Give it to me." Levy handed it over, with a word of warning: "Don't be thinking of no fancy doublecross, John. If you don't come back out of that bank with our million-six, don't come out at all."

But for once, Levy's tough-guy act wasn't particularly convincing—probably because his heart wasn't really in it. He was sure he would have his money in a matter of minutes, and he was just going through the motions with Davidson out of habit. Shinwell, he figured, certainly didn't bring him right to his bank if he wasn't planning on paying off. Levy and Bernstein stood in front of the bank grinning and nodding at each other like a couple of junior high school pranksters who had just tossed a cherry bomb into the principal's office and were waiting outside to hear the explosion and the ensuing cries of fear and confusion. But when Davidson hadn't returned in twenty minutes, Levy started to get nervous. "Where is he?" he asked Bernstein. "Where's our million-six? We should've checked the place for back doors. Those bastards might've snuck out the alley with our stock."

A few minutes later, Davidson walked out.

"Where's the money?" Levy demanded.

"Don't worry. The governor will be out in a minute. It takes a few moments to complete all the paperwork on a transaction of this magnitude."

"Yeah," Bernstein chimed in. "You can't just stuff a million-six in a paper bag. It takes a little while to get it all wrapped and counted."

That got Levy to thinking. Would Shinwell really give them that much cash? Suppose they got robbed? Maybe they should take a certified cashier's check instead. Or . . . ? Davidson returned to the bank.

After another ten minutes had passed, Shinwell and Davidson came out together. But neither of them was carrying anything.

"Where's the money?" Levy asked.

"You don't really want to carry all that cash around, do you?" Shinwell asked. "It could be rather dangerous. Why don't you let me have my bank Telex the money to your bank in Basel. The money will be there before you will. It will be much safer that way."

Levy thought a minute. "Okay. But I want a copy of the Telex."

Shinwell agreed. "I'll have to pay you in pounds, of course."

"Why?"

"Well, I'm British. My money is in pounds."

That sounded reasonable to Levy, and when Shinwell and Davidson returned to the bank, he and Bernstein began calculating the exchange rate from pounds to American dollars. They didn't know the exact rate of exchange, but they thought it was about $2.50 per pound (it was $2.40). "What's that—about six hundred thousand pounds?" Levy said to Bernstein. "Doesn't sound as good as a million-six, does it?" Bernstein admitted it didn't. "But it'll spend just as nice," he said. They both laughed.

As soon as Shinwell came back out, he thrust a copy of his Telex toward Levy. Playing his know-it-all role to the hilt, Levy looked at it, feigned a quick mental calculation and said, "You're a little short, aren't you, governor?" Actually, Levy hadn't the vaguest idea if the figure was right or not. But Shinwell glanced at the Telex, did some multiplication of his own and said, "I do believe you're right—about twenty-five thousand dollars short. No matter. We'll make it up on the next deal, right?" Levy said that would be okay with him. ("More than a million bucks in my pocket, and I'm gonna bitch about twenty-five thousand? Chickenfeed.")

They agreed to meet again in about thirty days to transact their next deal, and Levy and Bernstein—on cloud nine, with Davidson tagging along—raced back to their hotel to tell Hellmer and the Baron and Linda the good news.

"I can't believe we didn't get stopped by the cops," Levy says. "We were so happy, we drove like madmen. Traffic, pedestrians, red lights—nothing stopped us. We were crazy. Delirious. Out of our heads. When we got back to the hotel, we banged on the door and went into our rooms and we all jumped up and down on the beds and screamed and shouted. I fell on the floor and banged my ribs, but I didn't feel any pain. Me and the Baron are kissing each other, and I'm running out and dancing with the maid in the hallways. We're rich, rich—millionaires."

When the celebration died down, Levy lit up a cigar and suggested Bernstein call his banker in Basel to see if the Telex had arrived yet. The banker said it had arrived but there would be a temporary delay in making the cash available. The Telex was being rerouted through a London affiliate of Shinwell's bank since Shinwell had specified payment in pounds. The money would then be transferred from that bank to an affiliate of Bernstein's bank, also in London. When that transaction was complete, Bernstein's bank in Basel would honor the Telex and pay the money.

Levy thought that sounded rather odd, but the banker explained that Shinwell's bank was involved with Investors Overseas Services, the Bernie Cornfeld empire that was then undergoing worldwide upheaval. "With them, at this time, such precautions are necessary," the banker said, "but I wouldn't worry. I have heard nothing that would lead me to believe you shouldn't be able to collect your money here within forty-eight hours."

Bernstein seemed satisfied. Not Levy. He knew the story of Bernie Cornfeld and Investors Overseas Services only too well from having read the newspapers and talked casually with a few friends in Beverly Hills who knew Cornfeld. Anything involving Cornfeld looked like gold in 1969; by 1971, in Levy's words, "it looked like shit."

Cornfeld, once a Brooklyn social worker, has boasted that his billion-dollar international financial conglomerate would wreak an economic revolution, "converting the proletariat to the leisured class painlessly." His creation, he had said at the peak of his power, would become "the greatest single economic force in the Free World." For a while in the summer of 1969, with money pouring into his various mutual funds at the rate of $30 million a day, it looked as if Cornfeld might even have understated the case. Then his entire empire collapsed about his ears. In the first six months of 1970 alone, IOS lost $25 million. By the late spring of 1971—when Alan Levy was sitting in his hotel in Luxembourg, puzzling over the latest news from Bernstein's banker in Basel—Cornfeld had been unceremoniously ousted from control of his company, he had sold all his shares in the company and he was living in self-imposed, if not exactly Spartan, exile in his Beverly Hills mansion. "IOS," said three British journalists who had investigated it thoroughly, "was not a respectable financial institution. It was an international swindle." No wonder Levy was mightily distressed by the news from Basel.

He turned to Davidson, but before he could say anything, Davidson was saying, "Don't worry." Levy thought a minute. "Call Shinwell at his bank." Davidson called. Shinwell had already left. "Call his hotel." Davidson called. He'd just checked out. "What's his number in London, John?" Davidson said he couldn't reveal it. Levy grabbed him by the collar.

"Listen, you limey son-of-a-bitch, you better cough up his phone number *and* his address. If he's screwing me through some bankrupt bank, I'm gonna go to London and take my money out of his skin. If you don't wanna get yourself stuffed down a toilet, head-first, you better gimme that number right now."

Still Davidson refused.

Levy, as always when his bluffs of violence are called, backed off. "Okay, John, we're going to Dusseldorf. By the time we get there, his lordshit should be back in London. You get a hold of him there and tell him I want my money. No more bullshit. No more Telex. Cash money. Now. I don't care where he gets it or how he gets it—his affiliate, my affiliate, your affiliate, the King of Hungary's affiliate. I want my money."

Levy was so furious, he wouldn't even ride back to Dusseldorf with Davidson. "You go alone in your goddamn blue Cadillac. Me and Leonard and Ludwig and the Baron will rent our own car." Linda, it was decided, would return as she had come—alone.

On the ride back to Dusseldorf, Levy continued ranting and raving at his partners. He was sure Shinwell had taken the stock and stiffed them for the money. But the others disagreed. "I'm sure it's just a misunderstanding," Bernstein insisted.

"Misunderstanding?" Levy howled. "The only misunderstanding is that those two limey bastards are still alive. Well, I'll take care of that. I got a heavy back in L.A. He'll fix that Little Lord Fauntleroy. He'll tie him to the back of his Corniche and drag him through the streets of London for a million-six. He'll dump him in the English Channel. He'll . . ."

Levy was apoplectic. They had been so close to the money. It was practically in their pockets. They were counting it, spending it, reveling in it. Then this . . .

No one else seemed nearly as concerned as Levy, but no one had been through as much for the stock as he had. "Besides," he says, "I didn't know the other guys well enough to know if they really thought we'd still get the money or if they were just putting up a brave front. Ludwig didn't say much of anything the whole way back, for example, and I didn't know what to make of it. I figured he was pretty sharp, so he must have agreed with me. The only difference is Jews are so emotional. We're like the French and the Italians. We're always saying, 'I'm going to kill you. I'm going to strangle you. I'll cut your heart out.' The Germans don't bother with threats. They just do it. If they want to kill you, they don't scream and holler about it. They just take a gun out, blow your head off, put the gun back in their holster and finish their *schnapps.*"

Just outside Frankfurt, Levy pulled off the *autobahn* at a small dinner-house. While they were inside, John Davidson drove up and walked in. Bernstein suggested they invite him to join them. Levy wouldn't hear of it: "I hope he chokes to death on his food." Then he had a second thought: "But he shouldn't choke to death until he gives me Shinwell's address and phone number." Everyone at the table laughed. Even Davidson, who overheard the comment from several tables away—Levy's voice being about as soft as a thunderclap—had to hold his napkin to his mouth to keep from laughing out loud.

When they returned to Dusseldorf late that evening, they went straight to the Baron's apartment. Linda joined them there. So did Davidson—uninvited. Levy, as always, was glad to see Linda. He welcomed her help in translation, and he liked the way she carried herself. Sooner or later, he thought, her skills and knowledge would be of immense benefit to them all. Levy was not so pleased to see Davidson, but his presence reminded him of the $2 million in unnumbered stock they had given Davidson earlier.

"I want it back," Levy told him. Davidson said the stock was still at his girl friend's apartment, and he promised to deliver it the next day.

"I think your lordshit has had time to fly back to London by now, don't you, John?" Levy sneered. "Why don't you call him and ask him where our million-six is?"

Davidson went into the Baron's back bedroom and made his call. Apparently, he told Shinwell of Levy's threats because he came back into the living room a few moments later and told Levy, "The governor would like to speak with you." Levy bounded toward the telephone, but before he could say a word, Shinwell demanded to know, "How dare you threaten John?"

Levy erupted. "I ain't making no threats, governor, just promises. Now, you listen to me, you phony Earl of Girl or whatever the hell you are. You took my stock and left me with a piece of paper I can't even wipe my ass with."

Shinwell interrupted. "Calm down, will you please. You will remember that I told you when we first met that it would take forty-eight hours to clear everything." Now Levy interrupted.

"That was a different forty-eight hours. Don't try to con me, Ernie baby. I told you I got bad friends in the States. They'd as soon tear your throat out as look at you. Now you tell me when I'm going to get the money. You set the time. But it better be there. I've been stiffed on this stock a dozen times already, and I ain't letting you stiff me, too. If you don't want to see your wife and family dead, you get me my money. Now when can I get it?"

Shinwell said the money would be available in Bernstein's bank in Basel "within forty-eight hours—by Friday. Today's Wednesday." If the Telex didn't clear, he said, he would deposit fresh funds in London himself, and have it credited to Bernstein's account. Then he asked to talk to Davidson again. When they were through, Davidson again told Levy, "Don't worry. Everything's okay. Don't worry."

Bernstein and the Baron were certain everything was going to work out. The Baron, in particular, kept trying to reassure Levy—through Linda—that "the governor would not do this to us." When Levy remained unconvinced, the Baron excused himself and went back to his bedroom. He returned with a red leather case, about two feet long, a foot wide and three inches deep. It was lined in green velvet, and inside were two metal blow-guns and six darts.

The Baron repeated his feeling that Shinwell would make good on his end of the deal. "*Si non . . .*" As Linda translated—"If not . . ."—the Baron pointed to one of the blow-guns and the three darts alongside it and made a quick, blowing motion. Then he put his two hands together, palms facing, even with his right ear, and lay his head against them, closing his eyes and snoring, as if he were going to sleep—or mimicking someone put to sleep. Levy pointed to the other blow-gun and darts. The Baron grinned and made another blowing motion. Then he drew his right index finger quickly across his throat: "*Fini.*"

Levy just shook his head and laughed. The Baron, he knew by then, was big on threats and schemes. He was about as likely to use his blow-gun on Shinwell—or anyone else—as he was to climb the Eiffel Tower in the nude at high noon.

Before going to sleep that night, the men made their plans. Levy and Bernstein would fly to Zurich, rent a car and drive to Basel. Steve Berg, who was scheduled to arrive in Dusseldorf from Los Angeles the next morning, would accompany them as far as Zurich. Linda and the Baron would check into a hotel on the German side of the Swiss-German border, about twenty minutes from Basel, since the Baron risked arrest if he entered Switzerland. Hellmer would stay in Dusseldorf to collect the unnumbered stock from Davidson—and to keep an eye on Davidson . . . just in case the money wasn't in Basel.

The next morning, Levy picked up $900 he'd asked his mother to wire him. He also met Berg at the airport and told him there had been a slight delay: "We have to go to Switzerland for the money. You can come part way with us."

Levy wasn't surprised that Berg didn't ask to be in on the actual payoff in Basel. "He was still queasy about the whole thing. The less he actually saw, the better he liked it. He just wanted the money." Levy, of course, was delighted with that. He didn't want Berg around when the $1.6 million was discussed; Berg still thought the pot was only $600,000.

Before leaving for Zurich, Levy heard some discomfiting news. The Baron had been talking with a friend in Luxembourg, and the friend said there was talk in banking circles about a big stock swindle involving some Americans. But there were also reports that Shinwell had just consummated a big loan in Belgium, using $1 million worth of American stock as collateral. The Baron asked his friend if either Levy or Bernstein had been mentioned. The friend said he thought so, but he couldn't be sure.

Levy was unnerved—but not sufficiently unnerved to cancel the trip to Switzerland. "Anyone in his right mind would have crawled under a bed and hid for a month," he says. "Not me. I wanted to get to Basel as fast as my legs would carry me. I figured if Shinwell got a million bucks, he must be planning to pay us at least some of our money."

Levy, Bernstein and Berg flew to Zurich. It was late afternoon by the time they got Berg checked into the Ascot Hotel, and they knew they couldn't make the forty-five mile drive to Basel before the bank closed.

"The money's supposed to be there by tomorrow," Levy said. "Why don't you call now. Maybe it got there early."

Bernstein made the call. The banker spoke fluent German and French but only mediocre English. Still, he and Bernstein seemed to be communicating. Or so Levy assumed from Bernstein's end of the conversation:

"This is Mr. Bernstein. Has our money arrived yet? Oh good, it has. Fine, fine. We will see you in the morning then."

Bernstein hung up. "It's there."

Again—as he had twice before that same week, in Luxembourg—Levy began whooping with joy. He was exultant, ecstatic, euphoric. Berg wanted Levy to stay the night in Zurich, but now he couldn't wait to get to Basel. He and

Bernstein left immediately, taking a long, scenic route that trapped them behind a bicycle race and turned a sixty-minute drive into almost a four-hour drive. Not that either of them cared. For Levy, the excitement and satisfaction of a good swindle have strong sexual overtones. He even uses sexual terminology when he talks about it—"getting off," for example, is successfully completing a swindle—and on the drive to Basel that night, he was like a man in the most dreamily blissful of post-coital states . . . serene, beatific, surfeited. Levy has never taken drugs—not even marijuana—and he rarely drinks any liquor stronger than wine or an after-dinner cordial, but he speaks of the drive to Basel as "one long high—the kind of thing people must feel when they use drugs. It was better than a good shit, a good cigar and a good blow-job all rolled into one.

"A hustler like me spends his whole life dreaming of that one big score—the one score that's so big, you never have to make another score. You never have to worry again about whether you're doing right or wrong, legal or illegal. You never have to look over your shoulder. Is someone following you? The mob? The cops? The FBI? Are your partners screwing you? No more worries. No more finagling. No more having to stiff bookmakers. With my six-hundred-thousand-dollar share, I could come back to the U.S., give a good attorney fifty thousand to straighten things out and go live in a villa in Torremolinos for three or four years until things blew over, maybe even send my baby to school in Switzerland. Then I could come back to the United States and live like a king for the rest of my life. No, not like a king really. I didn't want a yacht or a big mansion or anything—just to be able to live well, comfortably, with security, and no worries ever again. No pressures. No bill-collectors. I could pay off 'Marty the Nose' and some other people I owed money to, and I'd still have about half a million bucks left for myself."

Levy and Bernstein talked that way on the entire trip to Basel. "Do you realize how much six hundred thousand dollars is?" Levy kept asking. "If you were a fancy-schmancy consultant who got paid two hundred fifty dollars a day, it would take you almost ten years to earn that much money. Six hundred thousand dollars. You could invest that in municipal bonds and get forty thousand dollars a year interest, tax-free, and never touch the principal."

Levy even had himself convinced he'd never gamble or hustle again. "I'd look for some new challenge. A score like this would prove I could do it. The excitement would be gone. I could never top it."

Of course, Levy thought, he would continue to supply Shinwell with the regular $2-million increments they had already discussed. That would net him almost $100,000 each time. And that wouldn't involve any risk. The groundwork had already been laid. He would just be fulfilling his commitment—like a Fuller Brush man delivering the goods a week after he'd made the sale.

In Basel, Levy and Bernstein checked into one of the city's best and oldest hotels, the Three Kings. They asked for the best, most expensive room available—a three-bedroom, two-sitting-room, two-bath penthouse suite with a balcony overlooking the Rhine River. Levy called his wife and told her to "go out and buy anything you want—we're rich." Then he and Bernstein ordered caviar, dinner, champagne and two women. Their tab for the evening was several hundred dollars. "But we could afford it. Who cares?"

They partied until five o'clock in the morning—interrupting the festivities only long enough to watch a Liza Minnelli special on television ("She's one of my favorites") and to shout out the window at some noisy antiwar demonstrators in the street below. At seven, they awoke in a semi-stupor, and bathed, shaved and dressed. An hour later, Linda knocked on their door. As planned, she and the Baron had driven from Dusseldorf to a small hotel just barely on the German side of the Swiss-German border,

and she had left him there to join Levy and Bernstein in
Basel. They told her about the banker's assurance that their
money was waiting for them that morning.

"Why don't you call the Baron," Levy suggested. "Let's
let him in on the good news."

Linda placed the call immediately, and even to two
listeners who didn't understand French, it was obvious from
her end of the conversation that both she and the Baron
were as thrilled by the news as Levy and Bernstein had
been.

Levy decided to call Hellmer in Dusseldorf, too. He
told him not to worry about Davidson any more and gave
him the name of the hotel in Zurich where Steve Berg was
staying. "Why don't you meet us there." Then they called
Berg. He said he didn't like his hotel; it was too old-
fashioned. He was moving to another one. They called
Davidson back and told him.

Shortly before nine, Levy, Bernstein and Linda left the
hotel by taxi for the bank. It was pouring rain, but Levy
insisted on jumping out of the cab en route to buy a new
briefcase—an $80, hand-tooled, all-leather briefcase. "I had
to have something to put all my money in, right? Me and
Leonard figured we'd each withdraw one hundred thousand dollars in cash for ourselves right then. We'd also get
the money for our partners. The rest of our shares we'd
leave in the bank awhile. Let them enjoy it. I mean, now
that we knew it was there, there was no hurry in withdrawing it all at once."

Levy, Linda and Bernstein arrived at the bank a few
minutes after it opened, and Bernstein asked for his banker.
A security guard picked up his telephone, announced their
arrival and directed them to an elevator. A second guard
joined them on the elevator. The security impressed Levy:
"When I'm getting ready to walk out of a bank with all
that cash, I like to know they're ready for me and want to
protect me."

The guard escorted them to a small office on the third floor of the bank. Someone would be with them in a moment or two, he said. Sure enough, within minutes, a bank official in a pin-striped suit and vest walked in.

Bernstein, carrying through on their previously agreed-upon ruse, showed the banker his portfolio of artwork and spoke in some detail of the sale he had just made. When he was through, he told the banker how much money they would be withdrawing that morning.

"But your money isn't here yet," the banker said.

Linda sat down heavily. Levy was near tears. Bernstein started to perspire. "What do you mean it isn't here? I spoke with you yesterday." The banker said he remembered the conversation, but all he had confirmed then was that the Telex was there. "Perhaps, it is my English. I am sorry if this misunderstanding has caused you any inconvenience. I hope you haven't delivered your artwork yet."

"Oh, of course not," Bernstein replied dumbly.

Levy looked up, muttering to himself: "What are they standing here talking about pictures for? Where's my money?" Then he decided the banker might try harder to get their money if he thought the pictures had already been delivered. He "reminded" Bernstein that they had, indeed, been delivered by then. The banker called Shinwell's bank in Luxembourg. The manager was in Paris for the day, and no one else there could help him.

"By this time," Levy says, "Leonard was sweating like crazy. It was like he was taking a shower. His light blue shirt was dark blue from the sweat. I told the banker we would try to clear things up ourselves, and I was sure he would have the money before the day was out."

The banker apologized again, and—it being Friday—offered to give them his home telephone number should they wish to speak with him over the weekend. Levy mumbled their thanks, and he and Bernstein and Linda took the elevator back down, hailed a cab and rode in silence back to the hotel.

Chapter 7

B ack at the hotel, Levy alternately played mobster and mother hen—threatening to kill Shinwell and worrying that Bernstein, still sweating, trembling and ashen, was on the verge of a heart attack. After they'd all calmed down, they called the Baron. His fury only reignited theirs. Levy called Davidson.

"John, you're a dead man. I don't care about my stock. I don't care about my million-six. For what you just put us through, you're a dead man. I don't give a fuck if you go hide in Denmark or Sweden or under a goddamn iceberg in the Atlantic. We'll find you and we'll kill you. Now you get a hold of that Little Lord Fauntleroy of yours, with his fuckin' gold buttons and his fuckin' decorations, and you tell him to get his ass on the phone to me."

Davidson insisted there must be a misunderstanding: "Don't worry."

Levy wasn't about to be mollified. "I don't give a fuck for your misunderstandings and your don't worry shit." He hung up.

Twenty minutes later, Davidson called back. "I just called the governor. He is in conference, but his wife will call you back in thirty minutes—at two o'clock."

At two exactly, the telephone rang. Bernstein answered it. Mrs. Shinwell identified herself, and Bernstein explained what had happened. Or, at least, he started to explain. Levy didn't much like the explanation. He thought Bernstein was being far too gentlemanly. Levy jerked the phone away and began shouting, his sense of outrage and injustice cascading forth like the violent retching of a dying man.

"Listen to me, you bitch. You tell that fucking sawed-off runt husband of yours that I'm going to have somebody come over there and suck his eyeballs right out of his head and drink every last drop of his blood."

Mrs. Shinwell was aghast: "Just who do you think you're talking to?"

"I'm talking to you, you fucking old douche-bag. I want my fucking money, and I don't care if your husband is meeting with the Queen. You tell him I want to talk to him. You tell him to call me."

He hung up.

Ten minutes later, the telephone rang. It was Mrs. Shinwell again. She'd spoken to her husband, she said, and the money would be in the bank within two hours—by four o'clock. As soon as it was deposited, she would call back. Levy wasn't convinced, but he had to wait. "Okay, asshole, I'll give you two hours. But I'm telling you right now, if the money isn't there, you're all dead Englishmen. I couldn't give a fuck for your Lord This-of-That and your John Davidson and your King John and your Magna Cartas and all that other British bullshit, including those two phony-baloney Corniches and that bankrupt bank. If I don't get my money, I'm gonna blow your fucking house up with all of you inside it."

Mrs. Shinwell protested that no one had ever spoken to her in that manner before.

"Well, someone's talking to you like that now. You're hearing it now. You better tell your husband about it. You tell him my friends in the United States are even worse than me. They'll cut his nuts off and serve them to the birds for breakfast. Remember, if my money ain't there, his lordshit might as well go dig a hole in the local grave-yard, 'cause I'm gonna throw dirt in his face."

Again Levy hung up.

For the next two hours, he snarled and snapped at every-one around him. Not even Linda, sitting silently in the corner, escaped his scorn. He told them he'd met a few "bad-ass musclemen" in Los Angeles, and he wasn't kidding about bringing one of them back to Europe with him. He knew just the right guy, he said, "cause we're about as likely to get our dough out of Shinwell as we are to be invited to Buckingham Palace to perform open-heart surgery on the Queen." When four o'clock came and went with no word from Mrs. Shinwell, Levy tried to call Davidson. No answer. They waited another hour. Still no Mrs. Shin-well. Still no Davidson. Still no money. They decided to go see the Baron. But they didn't have much money left to pay the hotel bill. When they got downstairs, Bernstein haughtily introduced himself to the cashier—"You know me, of course; I'm Leonard Bernstein." The cashier looked, wide-eyed, at Levy. "The maestro?" she asked. Levy, feign-ing diffidence, just shrugged: "Who else?" The hotel didn't accept TWA Getaway cards, but in the maestro's case, they said they would make an exception. Levy filed that piece of information in his fertile mind for future use, and he and Bernstein followed Linda across the Swiss-German bor-der to the hotel where the Baron was staying. It was, Levy says, sleazier than the sleaziest skid row hotel he'd ever seen.

"There was a strip-tease joint downstairs and little room upstairs where the girls took their tricks, and all over the walls, they had posters from some third-rate stag movies."

They went upstairs and brought the Baron up-to-date. He suggested they try to call Davidson again. After three tries, they finally reached him. "Okay, you rat bastard, where's my money?" Levy demanded. "I told you about my partners. They're on their way here now. They're gonna chop you up in little pieces unless you cough up the governor's address and telephone number." After ten more minutes of threats, each one more grotesque than the one before, Davidson surrendered the information.

Levy called Shinwell's number. Mrs. Shinwell answered. Levy didn't bother asking why she hadn't called back at four o'clock. Abuse and invective hadn't gotten him anywhere so far; he decided to try the calm approach. Speaking matter-of-factly, he told her he was in contact with his partners in the United States. They would be taking care of her and her husband. Meanwhile, John Davidson would be held hostage. He gave her the telephone number of the Baron's hotel. That was all. Goodbye.

Ten minutes later, the telephone rang. It was Shinwell. Bernstein answered. When it became obvious that Shinwell was doing most of the talking and Bernstein most of the listening—except for an occasional "Yes, Ernie"—Levy grabbed the receiver, his determination to remain calm now shattered.

"This is Alan, and I ain't no yes-Ernie man."

"Are you the one who talked so coarsely to my wife?"

"Oh, was that piece of shit your wife? For a million-six, I can talk to that douche-bag any way I please. Only talk ain't the half of it. You're both getting your brains blown out. How does that grab your limey ass? Are you still worried about how I talked to your wife, you fucking bullshit artist?"

Shinwell, seemingly unintimidated, warned Levy not to insult his wife or threaten either of them. "You will have your money Monday, I promise. I could have it for you tomorrow, but tomorrow is Saturday and the banks are closed."

Levy was certain by then that he would never see the money, and he told Shinwell so. Shinwell insisted they would be paid Monday. Levy said he would have to return to Zurich for a flight to Los Angeles anyway, so he would wait in Zurich until Monday. If the money weren't there, he would "go back to the States for my heavies."

Levy called Steve Berg in Zurich and told him what had happened. Then he dispatched the Baron and Linda to Dusseldorf to keep an eye on Davidson, and he and Bernstein drove to Zurich. They met Hellmer and Berg there, and Levy called attorney Martin Calaway in Beverly Hills. He thought Calaway might have some news about one of the other deals they had pending. Calaway had some news, all right, but it wasn't the kind of news Levy had hoped for. Calaway said Ralph Ernsten had heard through his FBI contact that two days earlier, on Wednesday, two men had been arrested in Geneva with International Chemical and Nuclear Corp. stock in their possession. Levy started to shake. "Geneva was only one hundred and thirty, maybe one hundred and forty miles from Zurich—a hop, skip and a jump away." He made a few calls to see if he could find any details.

"What happened was Mario Denard had seen some newspaper story that the chairman of the board of International Chemical and Nuclear was going to be in Geneva. According to the people I talked to, Mario got a brilliant idea. He called the guy from London and told him he had a million bucks worth of his stock. If the guy didn't pay him two hundred fifty thousand dollars for it, he said he'd flood the market with it and force the price down. That would cost the company a lot more than two hundred fifty thousand dollars. The chairman said he'd buy the stock and told Mario to come to Geneva with it. Mario got four buddies—a Frenchman and three Swiss—and the five of them go whistling off to Geneva like they really believe the chairman's gonna cave in that easy. Well, needless to say, when they step off the plane, the chairman's not there. But everyone else is—Interpol, the Swiss police, Freddie, Bernie and Irving, everybody."

Levy, for the first time since the stock caper began, was truly frightened. Shinwell hadn't paid him. The law was closing in. He was in a foreign country, almost seven thousand miles from home.

Levy, Bernstein and Berg went to the nearest Pan American Airways office to book passage home. They didn't have enough money for three round-trip tickets, so Bernstein pulled his "I'm Leonard Bernstein" routine again. But it didn't work this time. Berg volunteered to wire Gerry Kassap for $500. Then they checked out of their hotel; their reservation had only been good through Friday.

"We found another hotel for the weekend," Levy says, "but they only had one room for the three of us. They moved a bunk in with the twin beds."

On the way out of the hotel for dinner that night, Levy saw two Swiss police officers in the lobby. They were collecting passports, a routine practice in many Swiss hotels. But Levy didn't know that. He was sure they were after him. It was only a matter of time, he figured, before he'd be rotting the rest of his life away in a Swiss jail.

The $500 from Gerry Kassap arrived by wire the next day, and the three men bought their airplane tickets home. Berg also called his wife to tell her the flight number and arrival time so she could meet them at the airport.

The rest of the weekend was sheer hell for Levy, even though the hotel was a beautiful old building up in the mountains, near a clear, placid lake. He tried to walk and go for a boat ride, but he couldn't relax. He'd had almost a billion dollars worth of stock for almost five months, and all he had to show for it was the $1,250 from Bo Farmer in Phoenix and the $5,000 from Finn Konsmo in Orange County. He'd already spent at least twice that amount on travel and food, so instead of being rich, he was further in the hole than ever. And at any minute he expected to be arrested.

On Monday morning, an associate of Shinwell's called.

Shinwell, he said, would be calling shortly. Levy didn't wait. He called Shinwell's house. When Mrs. Shinwell answered, he put on his best Italian mobster accent. "This is Vito Cocavelli, lady. Where's your old man." Mrs. Shinwell asked "Cockavelli" who he was. "I'm one of Alan Levy's partners. I'm in Zurich now with Alan. You have your old man call me."

Thirty minutes later, Shinwell called. For the first time, he sounded worried. "Is Mr. Cockavelli there?" he asked. But Levy couldn't continue the charade. In his own voice, he said, "Okay, you shit, where's my money?" Shinwell said there had been a few complications—"you wouldn't understand, old boy"—but he was raising the necessary funds. Levy would be paid the next day. Levy wasn't listening. "Hey, asshole, you don't owe me the money any more. Every day it's tomorrow with you. I don't want your money, hear? I want your ass. I'm flying back to the United States tomorrow. I'll be back with a friend."

He hung up.

On the flight back to the United States, Levy and Bernstein discussed what they might do to raise some money.

They had both been amazed at how easily the "Leonard Bernstein" routine had worked in Zurich. Perhaps, if they selected their spots carefully, they could milk that for a lot of money. Maybe they could buy several pieces of expensive jewelry in Europe and sell it off in the United States. Bernstein said the ruse would probably work, but they might have to use checks, rather than "bleep-blops."

"That's what Leonard called credit cards—'bleep-blops.' That's the sound those little machines make when the salesclerk puts your credit card in and runs that thing back and forth over it. Bleep-blop. Leonard said he'd already spent more than his limit on several credit cards. That was why all those Germans had been screaming at him back in the Dusseldorf hotel lobby the first time I saw him. They were all merchants Leonard owed money to."

Levy, Berg and Bernstein landed in Los Angeles at 6:45 P.M. Tuesday, June 22. Gerry Kassap, anxious for his money, had been calling Berg's wife to find out when Steve would return home. As soon as she told him the flight number, he volunteered to save her a trip to the airport. "I'll pick him up," he told her.

When Levy and Bernstein saw Kassap standing near the international arrival gate, obviously waiting for them, they began cursing silently to themselves. They knew he would be upset that they still didn't have any money, and they were afraid that if Denard had been arrested in Geneva, the police might be tailing a few of their other partners in Los Angeles. Kassap took Levy and Berg to their homes, then dropped Bernstein off at the Century-Plaza Hotel in Century City. As soon as Levy walked into his house, his wife ran up to show him what she'd bought when he'd called from Luxembourg and told her to buy anything she wanted because they were rich.

"Fortunately, Frannie's not very extravagant. She could have bought diamonds, antiques, a new car, a whole houseful of furniture. What did she get? A purse, a purple purse. It cost eighty dollars, which is a lot of money for a purse, I guess, but when someone tells you you're going to be a millionaire and you can buy anything you want . . ."

Needless to say, Levy was grateful that Frannie hadn't bought something for $10,000; now he wasn't even sure he could pay for the $80 purse.

While Levy and his wife were talking about the purse, Kassap returned. When Levy opened the door to let Kassap in, he noticed a strange car parked across the street with two men in it, seemingly watching his house. He didn't know if he should pull Kassap inside, where they couldn't see, or if he should talk to him out front, where Frannie couldn't hear. He decided to take his chances outside, wondering all the while if he was becoming too paranoid. But what Kassap said soon confirmed his worst apprehensions. Kassap said he thought he was under police surveillance. When he hadn't heard from Levy for so long, he said, he'd made a few inquiries about peddling some stock elsewhere, through a girl he knew. The police had stopped the girl on another charge, and in the course of the investigation, she'd apparently led them to him. The previous day, Kassap said, he'd seen two men who "smelled like cops" parked across the street from his house.

Levy was furious. "So what the fuck are you doing here? You got cops tailing you, and you lead them straight to us? What kind of thinking is that? Why'd you even come to the airport? What are you gonna do, introduce them to us individually and invite them in for coffee and Danish?"

Kassap left after ten minutes. Later that night, Levy looked out the front window. The car was still there. He looked again—several times. It never moved. Finally, about five o'clock in the morning, unable to sleep, he decided to take a drive around the block—"just to see what they would do." They followed. In fact, they had to make such a quick U-turn to follow him that they almost hit another car. Levy roared with laughter. "It looked like the cops were the same kind of screwballs as my partners in crime. Right away I could see we'd all get along fine."

Levy decided to keep driving for a while. He'd look for a morning paper. Maybe there would be something in it about Mario Denard's arrest in Geneva. The other car followed him: He stopped; they stopped. He turned right; they turned right. He turned left; they turned left. He sped up; they sped up.

The next morning, Levy called Bernstein. "Something's up. Meet me at Calaway's."

At Calaway's office, Levy told Bernstein he was being followed. They asked Calaway what they should do. "There isn't much you can do," he told them.

On Thursday, Levy called Berg. Berg said he had some bad news—Kassap had just been arrested, and bail had been set at an inordinately high $100,000.

"Oh, oh," Levy said. "They're gonna squeeze him, scare the shit out of him. He'll never make bail, and they'll tell him he'll go to jail for life or some such shit if he doesn't talk. We're all dead."

A few hours later, Bernstein called Levy. He'd just heard from Linda in Belgium. She said the Baron had heard that Shinwell, an associate and a Swiss national had been arrested that morning in a Luxembourg bank with $7 million worth of stock in their possession.

Levy broke into a cold sweat. Denard had been arrested in Geneva. Kassap had been arrested in Los Angeles. Shinwell had been arrested in Luxembourg. The noose was getting tighter. How long would it be before they arrested him, too? But Bernstein said he didn't believe the story about Shinwell's arrest. "I think it's a smoke-screen. I think he put the story out to throw us off the trail. He figures if we think he's in jail, we won't bother coming back to Europe after our money."

Levy wondered how Shinwell could float such a story. "With his connections?" Bernstein asked. "Easy."

Levy couldn't decide whether to believe Bernstein's theory or his own fears. He made a quick check with several of his partners in the other stock deals. As usual, their deals were all "still in the works." Transactions that were supposed to have been completed in a matter of days had now dragged on for several weeks. No one mentioned any contact with police, though—and Levy didn't ask. "By then I figured everyone's phone was tapped," he says. "They made it sound like business-as-usual when I talked to them, but I wasn't taking any chances. I'd started out figuring I'd get rich and have to go to jail. Okay. Fair trade. But now it was beginning to look like I wasn't going to get rich and I might have to go to jail anyway. I didn't much like that idea. That's no trade; that's a screwing."

Levy told Bernstein he'd contact the strongarm friend he'd mentioned while they were in Europe. "If Shinwell is out, I want my million-six. I may be going to jail, but after all this shit, I'm not going without some dough buried in a hole somewhere for when I get out."

Levy's strongarm friend, Tony Bruno, lived in a duplex in West Los Angeles. Levy called and arranged to see him the next day.

"The next thing I knew, Steven called me again and said Kassap's bail had been reduced to three thousand or five thousand or something like that, and he was out of the can. That only meant one thing to me—he'd talked. I had to move fast."

Early the next morning, Levy went to see Tony Bruno. Bruno was primarily a burglar, and he had, quite literally, the guts of a burglar. Once he'd stolen a huge brass vase from the front entrance of the Plaza Hotel in New York in broad daylight just to prove it could be done. As a final fillip to the prank, he'd dumped the vase on the front lawn of a home owned by mobster Albert Anastasia, who had once said, only half in jest, that he'd like to have one of the vases for his porch. Another time, Bruno had stolen a beautiful Persian rug from the floor of a Manhattan movie theater—while it was open—by pretending to be from a rug-cleaning company. He had just rolled the rug up, brushed the manager aside and walked off with it.

But Bruno had more than guts going for him. He had the one indispensable quality for any successful criminal—an utter disregard for the law and for his own safety. He would do what he wanted, when he wanted, and damn the consequences. Just under six feet tall, with dark, sunken eyes and a perpetual snarl on his lips, he looked the part of a strongarm. He was, in fact, just then out on bail on an armed robbery charge. He'd put the barrel of a .38-caliber revolver in a woman's mouth, and told her to give him her jewels "or I'll blow your head off." He got the jewels.

That was the kind of man Levy wanted to take back to see Shinwell.

Levy asked Bruno if he would have any trouble leaving the country. Bruno shook his head. Often, when a suspect is out on bail, his bond is made contingent on his promise not to leave the country—or even, sometimes, the state. On occasion, authorities may require him to surrender his passport as a condition of bail. But no such requests or restrictions had been imposed on Bruno. He was free to come and go as he pleased, just so long as he didn't miss his next court date.

"Good," Levy said, and he started to tell Bruno about Shinwell. Bruno had a couple of stories he wanted to share with Levy first, though. He'd recently been involved in a couple of jobs that gave him special pleasure, and—as one raconteur to another—he couldn't wait to tell Levy all about them. One had been an attempted burglary of an office in Manhattan. Bruno and his partners had been unable to break in through the ground floor of the building, so they'd broken into the building next door instead. They went up twenty-five stories, jimmied the lock on an office door and opened a window that looked out on their target building. Then they lowered Bruno out the window by rope.

"They were gonna swing me back and forth," he told Levy. "The two buildings were pretty close. We figured they could swing me up against the other building and I could get in through a window. Usually those big buildings aren't as careful about locking the windows on the floors above street level."

Bruno paused, enjoying the role of expert and lecturer-in-residence.

"We had only one problem. I'm up there, maybe ten stories or so above Madison Avenue, and all of a sudden, I hear this goddamn ripping sound. It's my pants. The goddamn crotch of my pants are ripped and my nuts are waving in the breeze ten stories over Madison Avenue. The two guys holding the rope were laughing so hard, they almost let go. I don't know what scared me the most—falling or having pneumonia of the balls."

Levy laughed appreciatively over the story, then tried to introduce the Shinwell matter.

"Wait a minute, wait a minute," Bruno said. "One more." And he went on to tell about a car swindle he'd just run:

"It was pretty simple really. We'd find guys who were greedy enough to want a new car cheap and not care much where it came from. We'd take their order, steal the car off the docks or out of some lot and sell it to them cheap." He laughed. "We could afford to sell cheap; we didn't have much overhead."

His most recent sale, Bruno said, had been to a dentist.

"The guy wanted a blue Coupe de Ville. He said it had to be blue. No other color would do. But me and my partner looked all over New York. We couldn't find one. Finally, I said we'd steal any Coupe de Ville we could find, and I'd paint the son-of-a-bitch blue. We did it. De-livered the car right to the guy's office. Know what he does? Tries to screw us on the price. We'd agreed on a price, and he held back seven hundred dollars. He didn't know exactly how we got the car, but he knew enough to be pretty sure we couldn't go squawking to the cops or the Better Business Bureau."

Bruno accepted the dentist's money after only a token complaint. That night, the dentist called him. "You wouldn't believe what happened to me," the dentist said. "When I went out to my car after my last patient, it wasn't there. Someone stole it."

Bruno clucked sympathetically, hung up, and walked outside and drove off in his new car . . . a blue Cadillac Coup de Ville.

Again Levy laughed. Again he tried to talk about the stock. This time Bruno listened. But Levy decided not to tell him too much.

"Tony was a friend," he says. "I didn't see any reason to expose him to the cops. The less he knew, the less trouble he could get in. I figured he could probably get my money for me without any real violence—just threaten the guys some, you know? With his mug and the way he acted, I figured they'd have tobacco stains in their pants in thirty seconds, and I'd have my money in sixty seconds. I just told Tony the telephone number—a million-six. I knew that would be enough to get him interested. I promised him a good piece of the action plus all his expenses."

They agreed to leave within a week.

That afternoon, Bernstein came to see Levy. "Shinwell's bank is supposed to be closed," he said. "I just heard from Linda. Maybe it's more bullshit, like the jail story. I don't know."

They decided to get back to Europe as quickly as possible to see for themselves what had happened to Shinwell and his bank—as well as to John Davidson and the un-numbered stock his girl friend was still holding. While they were there, they figured, they might need some cash. Levy borrowed more from his mother, and he and Bernstein worked out a plan for trying to buy some jewelry to sell when they returned. They even consulted an attorney on it. He assured them they wouldn't be prosecuted for passing bad checks in Europe. "Just make sure you get back here before the checks bounce. It takes twenty-six days for a check to clear from Europe, and if you're back here by then, you're home free. They'll never extradite you, and they'll never prosecute you."

Levy couldn't believe his ears. It sounded like a license to steal. He asked the attorney to check with someone in the district attorney's office. He did. Same story. No prosecution was likely. Things were looking up. Levy called Linda, put $100 in a checking account in West Los Angeles, then headed for the airport with Bernstein. They used his Pan American Airways credit card to buy three tickets to Dusseldorf.

The next day, exactly a week after his return to Los Angeles from Europe, Levy had a visitor in his Cheviot Hills home. It was the white chauffeur who had driven movie producer Tom Wilson around. Wilson, the chauffeur said, had been arrested. The chauffeur said he liked Levy, and thought Levy might want to know what had happened. Levy thanked him, but didn't waste much time on gratitude. Wilson. Denard. Kassap. Shinwell. *If* Shinwell really had been arrested. And that doctor, Fats Jackson's friend—maybe he hadn't been lying about the FBI coming to his house. Levy wondered if he'd be able to leave the country before the police closed in. "For all I knew, the FBI would nail me at the airport," he says. But no one stopped him, and he and Bernstein and Bruno flew to London to make connections to Dusseldorf. Between planes, on an airport shuttle bus, Levy and Bernstein got a foretaste of Bruno's infantile crudity. "There was an old Russian woman on the bus," Levy says. "She must have been ninety if she was a day. Tony got the idea she was a Russian and he walked up to her and said, 'Hey lady, you a Rusky?' She muttered something in Russian. Tony glared down at her and said, 'Khrushchev, Brezhnev, phooey.' Then he acted like he was gonna strangle her. She started screaming and Tony cracked up laughing. Great, huh? We're trying to dodge Freddie, Bernie and Irving, and our big hitman is creating an international mob scene."

Chapter 8

When Levy, Bernstein and Bruno landed in Dusseldorf, Linda and the Baron met them at the airport. The three Americans checked into the Esplanade Hotel—"my home away from home," Levy calls it—then joined Linda and the Baron at his apartment. John Davidson, the Baron said, had left Dusseldorf the minute he got word Levy was coming back. "He's probably in England," the Baron said. "Why don't I go look for him?"

The next morning, Linda and the Baron flew to London. There was no trace of Davidson there either, so they returned to Dusseldorf.

"We figured Davidson wouldn't show his face in Dusseldorf as long as he thought me and Leonard and Tony were around," Levy says. "We decided we should leave and be ready to send Tony back in a hurry when John showed up."

Levy still couldn't confirm the story of Shinwell's arrest, though. Everyone he talked to seemed to think it was true, but no one knew for sure. He and Bernstein decided they'd better not rely on the money they had coming from Shinwell. It was time to try the jewelry caper.

"The Baron didn't think we should try anything," Levy says. "The way he talked, we had every police force in the world looking for us—Interpol, the FBI, the Swiss police, the International Arab police, the French Foreign Legion, everyone. He said we should lock ourselves in his apartment and hide under the bed. But me and Leonard didn't want to go home empty-handed, not after all we'd been through on the stock."

They discussed the arguments for and against the jewelry scam for several hours, but it was clear that Levy had irrevocably made up his mind. Before long, he wasn't even participating in the discussion. He was just staring out the hotel window with that dreamy, faraway look he always gets in his eyes when he thinks a big score is within his grasp.

The next day, Levy and Bernstein walked along the main street of Dusseldorf, systematically examining all the jewelry stores. They wanted to hit an expensive store, a store that carried extremely valuable jewelry, so they could make the biggest possible killing on the fewest possible purchases. They also wanted to make sure the store didn't accept credit cards; otherwise, the store might be reluctant to accept their checks. "They'd just tell us to use our credit cards instead," Levy says.

Finally, after several hours of walking and looking and thinking and talking, Levy and Bernstein settled on the Wyersberg Jewelry Company. It was one of the few jewelry stores they saw that didn't have credit card decals on the front window.

"We were very careful about how we dressed," Levy says. "We didn't go in all spiffed out in suits and ties or anything like that. We dressed Beverly Hills casual. We'd found that saying you're from Beverly Hills impresses people even more in Europe than it does in the United States. Tell a European you're from Beverly Hills and you can forget about it; you gotta be a movie star or a multimillionaire for sure. You get a free pass to everything. So we dressed the part. I'm wearing white Levis and a navy-blue, alligator shirt and a navy windbreaker—and tennis shoes. Leonard and Tony both dressed about the same."

When Levy and Bernstein walked into the Wyersberg Jewelry Company, the first man they saw was a security guard—"a guy about five-foot-five, sixty years old, built like a bowling ball," Levy says. Standing just behind the guard inside the store was a tall, slender, blond man in a suit and white shirt and tie. Levy walked up and said he'd like to see some jewelry. But the man didn't speak English too well. He excused himself and introduced Levy to a salesgirl who spoke English fluently. Levy introduced Tony Bruno as his brother-in-law. "And this," he said, nodding to Bernstein, "is Mr. Leonard Bernstein." The salesgirl's eyes opened wide. "*The* Leonard Bernstein?" she asked. Levy shrugged: "Of course." The salesgirl huddled with the man who had first greeted Levy. The man apparently was her boss. When she returned, she was all smiles. She put away a tray of jewelry she had been about to show Levy, and brought out another tray from the back of the store.

"You could see right away it was the real good stuff, the stuff they saved for their richest customers," Levy says. "But before I could start to talk to her about what we wanted, I noticed that Tony was off by himself, wandering around the store, stealing things left and right. The fat old security guard didn't see anything, but I sure as hell did. Tony was dropping watches and necklaces in his pocket like crazy."

Levy excused himself and walked over to Tony. "Put 'em back," he hissed. "We'll get all we want with checks." Reluctantly, Bruno complied.

While Levy and Bernstein were looking at several men's watches, another gentleman introduced himself. He was, he said, the son-in-law of Herr Wyersberg, the proprietor. He and the salesgirl both asked what Mr. Bernstein was doing in Dusseldorf. Levy replied that they were visiting their friends, en route to Paris, where they would be meeting with Otto Preminger, the film director. "I'm a producer. We're all going to Spain to make a movie." That seemed to impress both of them.

Levy selected three pieces of jewelry—two women's watches and one man's watch. Both women's watches were diamond-studded Chopards; the best of them had a seventeen-jewel Swiss movement, an Australian fire opal dial and a bracelet of eighteen-carat white gold, with ninety-eight single-cut diamonds. Bernstein also selected a woman's Chopard watch. It had thirty-two diamonds. Then he asked, "Could you help me select a ring for my wife, something in a sapphire or emerald?" Wyersberg's son-in-law escorted him to a case where the precious stones were displayed. "We have a gorgeous emerald, Herr Bernstein," he said. The ring was a square-cut emerald, about ten carats, absolutely magnificent. Bernstein whistled appreciatively. "I'll take it."

Bernstein's ring and watch coast $10,800. Levy's three watches cost $3,361.

"Do you take credit cards?" Bernstein asked, reaching for his wallet.

"Nein."

Levy, meanwhile, was already writing a check for his purchase. "A check is fine, I presume?" he asked.

"Certainly. For Mr. Bernstein, a check is the same as cash."

Tony Bruno, standing silently aside during all the buying, almost gagged. Levy silenced him with a glare, and handed his passport to Wyersberg for identification. While the jewelry was being wrapped, the guard went upstairs. He returned with an older man. The salesgirl spoke briefly with the old man, in German, then said, "Herr Bernstein, I should like you to meet Herr Wyersberg, the proprietor."

Levy beamed. "The old guy is smiling at his son-in-law, and I'm thinking that he's thinking what a good job they've done screwing us Jews. Probably marked everything up twenty-five percent on us. But I figure we'll show the Kraut bastards. We just stuck it up their ass and broke it off. They can't even call our bank in L.A. to see if the checks are any good. We've got the nine-hour time difference working for us. During business hours in Dusseldorf, it's the middle of the night in L.A."

When the jewelry was ready, Levy told Wyersberg, "Everything you've shown us is so beautiful, we would like to buy some more. Unfortunately, we have to leave this evening for Paris—we'll be staying in a penthouse suite at the Paris Hilton—and we have so many other things to do. Do you have a catalog of any sort that we might glance through at our convenience? Perhaps we could call you from Paris and order some more. I'm sure that when we tell the rest of the people on our movie about all you've done for us, they'll want to order some, too. Mr. Preminger, in particular, is a lover of fine jewelry. Of course, we also like to buy a few smaller gifts when we're through with a picture. We give them to some of the behind-the-scenes people who've been so helpful."

Wyersberg's son-in-law said he would be delighted to provide a few pictures. He gave Levy a stack of them, each showing a single piece of jewelry and listing the description and price of the piece on the back.

"If we don't see what we want here, may we just call you back with a general idea of what we have in mind?" Levy asked. "I trust we can leave the final selection to your discretion then."

"Certainly. I will select for you the most elegant and sophisticated jewelry we have. Just place your confidence in me."

Before they left the store, the salesgirl asked Bernstein for his autograph. He gave it to her—with a flourish—and when he and Levy and Bruno walked out, they were struggling against the temptation to break into laughter—or into a dead-run. "Come on," Levy said. "Let's get checked out of the hotel and go to the airport before those clowns realize what we did to them."

The three men walked straight to an airline ticket office to book their flight to Paris. The ticket-seller wanted cash. Bernstein showed her his TWA credit card. It had expired three months earlier, but before the girl behind the counter could either check it or refuse it, he opened his briefcase and flung a whole assortment of credit cards at her. The ensuing scene, Levy says, was hilarious.

"He had Shell and Mobil and Texaco and all the Vegas casino credit cards and just about every department store credit card you can name. None of them are any damn good to buy airline tickets, of course, but the poor girl didn't know what to say in that blizzard of credit cards. She just had to figure that any guy with that many cards had to be a good credit risk—especially if his name was Leonard Bernstein. She gave us the three tickets to Paris without checking his TWA card at all."

Before leaving for Paris, Levy talked to the Baron and Linda. She was returning to Brussels, she said. Levy and his friends should stop by and visit her before they returned to the United States. They could lie low for a couple of days while she checked around to see how close the law was.

"Good idea," Levy said. "We'll come there after Paris. Maybe John Davidson will be back in Dusseldorf by then, and we can send Tony back to take care of him and find out about Shinwell."

Levy, Bernstein and Bruno checked into the Paris Hilton —a penthouse suite, of course, with three bedrooms, four baths and a large living room.

"We registered under Leonard's name," Levy says. "They couldn't do enough for us. They sent up wine and fresh fruit and flowers and hors d'oeuvres, and we had a TV in every room. The suite cost something like three hundred dollars a night. What did we care? We weren't paying for it. We'd use one of Leonard's bleep-blops."

The next morning, Levy called the Baron. Good news. Davidson was back in Dusseldorf, and he was coming in to the Baron's office the following day. Levy and Bernstein hustled Bruno to Orly Airport. Bernstein ordered Bruno a ticket from Paris to Dusseldorf to Brussels, where they would all rendezvous.

"How would you like to pay for this?" the girl behind the Lufthansa ticket counter asked.

"With my TWA Getaway card," Bernstein replied.

"We don't take TWA Getaway cards," the girl said.

Bernstein offered his Pan American Airways credit card. Same answer.

"We accept Diners Club and American Express," the girl said.

Bernstein had neither. He went into his haughty maestro act. "What are you questioning me for? Don't you realize who I am? I am Leonard Bernstein. Forget all those credit cards. Charge it to me personally." With that, he opened his briefcase and flung his sheaf of credit cards at her. The girl started to cry. "I'll have to get the manager," she said, scurrying off.

"She went back to a glass window and knocked on it," Levy says. "The manager comes out and she introduces him to Leonard. Leonard says he can't understand what all the fuss is about. 'You don't take TWA,' he says, 'and you don't take Pan Am and you try to tell me what credit cards I should carry. Well, I have all these.' And he throws the pile of cards at the manager."

But the manager wasn't intimidated.

"I don't care who you are," he says, "don't throw your credit cards at me."

Bruno, who'd been itching for action ever since he left Los Angeles, stormed into the melee. "Hey, you Nazi son-of-a-bitch, who you screaming at?" The manager backed off. Bruno lunged toward him. The manager ran toward his office. Bruno squeezed under the counter, chased the man into his office and grabbed him by the throat. Levy and Bernstein, clawing wildly at Bruno's shirt, managed to pull him off.

"The ticket was only about fifty dollars," he says. "For fifty dollars, we didn't have to get arrested and thrown in a German jail. We paid for the ticket in cash and sent Tony on his way."

The next morning, when John Davidson walked into the Baron's office, Bruno was sitting there waiting for him. Davidson, always the proper Britisher, introduced himself: "How do you do, old chap? Nice meeting you."

Bruno bolted from his chair, grabbed Davidson by the tie and jerked the tie as tight as it would go. "Fuck your old chap crap, you goddamn limey asshole. I'm Alan Levy's friend from the States. Where's the merchandise, where's the dough and where's Shinwell? Fast. I ain't Alan. I won't take all that bullshit you gave him." Davidson, his eyes bulging, tried to talk. Bruno jerked the tie even tighter. Davidson got red in the face. He started gasping for breath. The Baron had to pull Bruno off him.

Davidson was cringing in a corner, terrified. He stammered that the governor was in jail and the police had the stock. Bruno hit him in the mouth. Davidson still insisted Shinwell was in jail. Bruno decided he was telling the truth. "Where's the merchandise?" (meaning the unnumbered stock). Davidson said he had it. "I'll go get it." He got up to leave. Bruno tripped him.

"Wrong again, asshole. I told you I'm not Alan. You're married to me now. *You* won't go get the stock. *We'll* go get the stock. Okay, asshole, move!"

On the way out, Bruno called Levy in Paris, and told him what Davidson had said. Levy was puzzled. What about the loan Shinwell was supposed to have made in Belgium? he wondered. Perhaps Shinwell had completed that transaction before the police caught him and took the rest of the stock. Where was that money? Levy thought a minute. There wasn't much he could do just then about Shinwell, the stock or the Belgian loan. The Tom Wilson stock was gone, too; the police had confiscated that when they arrested Mario Denard in Geneva. Maybe one of the other deals—Mr. Todd or the Phoenix loan or the Hume Cannery—would come through. But everyone was probably lying low. The best thing for him to do would be to destroy the unnumbered stock Davidson was holding. That was the strongest physical evidence linking him to the rapidly fizzling stock swindle. Whether he was arrested or not, he could always try to peddle the rest of the stock again later. He told Bruno to burn the stock as soon as he got it from Davidson.

"That's exactly what he did, too," Levy says. "He took it out in an open field and poured lighter fluid all over it and tossed a match on it. More than two million dollars' worth of unnumbered stock, all gone up in flames. Damn near burned Tony, too. The fire singed all the hair on his head."

When he was through, Bruno reported back to Levy. "I wanna go to Luxembourg and get Shinwell," he said. "I'll go right into the goddamn jail after him." Levy said that wasn't possible. Bruno was like a wild animal denied his raw meat. "That's what you brought me all the way over here for, isn't it? I'm supposed to squeeze the money out of Shinwell, right? I can't do that if he's in Luxembourg and I'm in Dusseldorf." Levy didn't know what to say. Finally, he told Bruno, "Look, we probably got half the cops in the world on our tails already. A jailhouse murder we don't need. Me and Leonard may have a good thing going with the jewelry. Why don't you meet us in Brussels like we planned. We'll catch up with Shinwell later. A guy with connections like he has won't be in jail long. When he gets out, we'll be waiting for him."

Bruno didn't much like the idea of waiting, but he agreed. He said he'd see Levy and Bernstein in Brussels.

Bruno's message on Shinwell didn't depress Levy quite as much as it might have before his visit to the Wyersberg Jewelry Company. He had pretty much written his million-six off by then anyway—subconsciously, if not consciously. He'd spread more than $15 million worth of stock around the world, and he still had nothing to show for it. But there was plenty more where that came from, and the jewelry buy in Dusseldorf had been so easy, he could probably do that a few more times in various European cities. He wouldn't make millions on the jewelry, but he should be able to clear $50,000 on it, maybe $100,000— maybe more. With that kind of cushion, he could dodge the law for a while, then start all over with the stock when the heat was off. Besides, who could be depressed in a penthouse suite in the Paris Hilton.

That afternoon, Monday, July 5, the Wyersberg Jewelry Company called the Bernstein suite while Levy and Bernstein were eating lunch. It was one of the gentlemen they had spoken to when they were in the store, and he wanted to speak to Bernstein. Levy said he was "in conference with Mr. Preminger on a very sensitive matter relating to the score of our film." The jeweler said he would hold. Levy, loving every minute of the charade, said that would be just fine. He put the telephone receiver under a pillow on the sofa and finished eating his lunch, assuming the jeweler would get tired of waiting after a few minutes and hang up. While they ate, he and Bernstein sorted through the Wyersberg pictures, choosing the pieces of jewelry they thought they could make the best profit on when they returned to Los Angeles. Twenty minutes later, when they were through eating, Levy retrieved the receiver to hang it up. But he heard someone calling "Hello, hello?" on the other end.

"Are you still there?" he asked. "I'm sorry. I must have

forgotten you called. Mr. Bernstein is free now. He can speak with you."

Bernstein picked up the phone, and the jeweler asked him to please call him by his first name—"Hans or Fritz or Wolfgang or whatever it was," Levy says. Bernstein replied: "Fine. You may call me Mr. Bernstein." Had Mr. Bernstein decided on any more jewelry? the man from Wyersberg wondered. He had indeed. Bernstein started ordering—for himself, for Levy and for "Otto Preminger." Among the items he ordered for himself were an eighteen-carat white gold woman's bracelet with eighty-five brilliant-cut diamonds and 102 marquise-cut diamonds. It cost $10,500. He also ordered an eighteen-carat white gold brooch with sixty brilliant-cut diamonds and sixty-eight marquise-cut rubies; a platinum and eighteen-carat white gold ring with a four-carat ruby and eighty brilliant-cut diamonds, and a platinum and eighteen-carat white gold bracelet with five rubies and eighty brilliant-cut diamonds. His total bill was $35,230.

Levy ordered a platinum and eighteen-carat white gold bracelet with forty-five brilliant-cut diamonds, and a ring with fourteen emeralds and twenty-nine brilliant-cut diamonds. His total bill was $15,941.

Bernstein told the jeweler to mail the jewelry to his home in Los Angeles. "We will not be back in Dusseldorf soon," he said. The jeweler suggested sending the jewelry to them "on location in Spain." Bernstein brushed the idea aside. "No, no. It is better if you send it directly to the United States. You know the Spanish mails. They're not like the German mails at all—not the least bit reliable." The jeweler agreed. He also agreed to minimize the actual value of the jewelry so they wouldn't have to pay as much duty. Bernstein said their checks would be in the mail soon.

When he hung up, Levy turned to Bernstein. "Leonard, do you think the guy will really send all that stuff? We're into him for better than sixty-five grand now."

Bernstein said he was sure the jeweler would fill their orders. "Why shouldn't he? He figures he's already got better than fourteen grand in his pocket—the two checks we wrote for the stuff we bought in Dusseldorf."

Levy nodded. "The greedy son-of-a-bitch. He probably will send the stuff. He may even call us again to see if we want to order more."

When Levy and Bernstein checked out of the hotel in Paris, they arranged a little scenario. They had stayed in the Hilton because they knew most Hiltons accept a TWA Getaway card, and that's what Bernstein planned to pay their bill with. But if there was any trouble at the cashier's cage, he told Levy, "you just head for the airport. I'll meet you there."

Levy called a bellman to take their luggage downstairs. He was to have the luggage loaded in a taxi and wait ten minutes—no more—for Bernstein. But hotel regulations prohibited guests from loading their luggage until they had checked out, paid their bills and been cleared by the cashier. The bellman stacked the luggage—six bags in all—alongside a taxi. Levy waited five minutes, ten minutes. Bernstein didn't come out, and Levy—with his luggage still piled in front of the hotel entrance—couldn't leave. He walked gingerly back into the hotel, hoping to catch sight of Bernstein without himself being seen. He need not have been so cautious. Bernstein spotted him immediately, and screamed for him to come to the cashier's window.

Playing the maestro role again, Bernstein treated Levy like his secretary. "Do you realize," he snapped, "that you did not pay our TWA bill, and now they will not accept my TWA card on our bill here?" Levy caught on right away. He knew the card was no good, but he apologized most abjectly for this shameful neglect of his duties. "I'm so sorry, maestro. Please forgive me."

Bernstein turned imperiously to the cashier. "He is my personal secretary. The help these days." He shook his head.

"I just don't know what I'm going to do about him. Well, you'll have to send the bill to me personally, at my home. You have my address from the registration forms, I believe."

The cashier said she was sorry for the embarrassment and the inconvenience, but she had to insist on full payment in cash—"even from Leonard Bernstein." Bernstein drew himself up to his full five feet eleven inches and said, "Well, if my personal credit is not good here, I'm leaving." With that, he wheeled, pushed Levy toward the door and began to march out.

"As we left," Levy says, "the cashier started screaming, 'Mr. Bernstein, Mr. Bernstein.' She had to walk down the full length of the counter to get to us, and while she was doing that, we grabbed our luggage and started stuffing it in the taxi. It was like a scene out of Laurel and Hardy. She's screaming 'Mr. Bernstein, Mr. Bernstein' and the bellman is screaming for the *gendarmes* and the doorman is tooting his whistle like a maniac and trying to pull the luggage out of the cab while Leonard and I are putting it in. On top of everything, the hotel is busier than hell. It's a Monday, the first week in July, and the lobby is just jammed with tourists, all of whom have to think we're crazy. All the while this is going on, Leonard is telling the cabdriver, 'Orly Airport, Orly Airport, *vite vite.*'

"Finally, a cop walks up from the corner. Naturally, he doesn't speak English. By this time, the cashier is outside yelling at all of us. She tells the cop we're trying to skip out on our hotel bill. We try to explain that it's all a misunderstanding, that they had agreed to send us the bill later. The cop isn't listening to us, though, and we have to go back in and settle up. We empty our pockets and our briefcases and everything. It takes damn near every penny we have left. Thank God, Leonard had a few franc notes left in his wallet. We used that to pay the cabbie when we got to the airport."

But even then, Levy couldn't relax. The more he thought

about flying to Brussels, the less he liked it. Belgium was too close to Luxembourg, where Shinwell had been arrested. The police might be waiting for him. They might have Linda's house staked out already. "I don't like it," he told Bernstein. "I got a feeling the cops are just one step behind us. I don't like it. The whole thing's gonna blow up on us any minute—the stock, the jewelry, everything." Bernstein told Levy he was exaggerating their predicament. "Don't worry, Alan. Nobody wants us. It's all bullshit. We could stay in Europe for the rest of our lives."

Levy wasn't convinced. Still, he *could* use a couple of days' rest, and Linda's place might be just right for it. There were supposed to be several fine jewelry stores in Brussels, too. Maybe he could pick up a few more rings and watches and bracelets. No sense wasting the trip.

When they landed in Brussels, Bernstein flashed his passport and walked through Customs unmolested. But when Levy approached, the man in charge of the Customs desk glanced at him as if he recognized him. Then he started flipping through a large book of photographs. Levy's heart fell. The book, he assumed, had pictures of wanted men. Obviously, he was in it. This was it. The caper was over. Just then, Tony Bruno walked up. He had come to the airport to meet them, as previously arranged, and he could see Levy might be in trouble. He bulled his way through the crowd, grabbed Levy by the shirtsleeve and said, "C'mon, we gotta go."

"Wait a minute, Tony. I have to get my passport back from this guy."

Bruno glared at the Customs man. "Hey you, give my friend his passport."

The Customs man said he had to check something first.

"Whaddya mean check? Who you think this is, John Dillinger? Whaddya think you're pulling anyway? What kind of dump is this? I'm an American and he's an American and we don't have time for all this shit."

He jerked the passport out of the Customs man's hand,

shoved Levy ahead of him and stalked toward the door. The Customs man just sat there, flabbergasted. He didn't say a word. He didn't move a muscle. Levy, Bernstein and Bruno took a taxi to the Brussels Hilton, where Bruno had made their reservations in Bernstein's name. Once again, they got the VIP treatment—champagne, fresh fruit and flowers in their suite. They settled in and called Linda. If they had any doubts about Shinwell having been arrested and imprisoned, she set them to rest. "It's true, absolutely true," she said. "I checked it out myself."

That night, over champagne and dinner, the three Americans listened to a baseball game over Armed Forces radio. "It was Pittsburgh against the Giants," Levy says. "Tony even tried to get a bet down on it, but with the time difference, he couldn't reach his book in the States in time."

The next morning, Linda met them at the hotel, and they all walked into a jewelry store. Levy selected several watches. But the saleswoman said she couldn't give him the watches until she had called their bank to verify the check. They all walked out—quickly. Bernstein laughed. "I'm glad somebody in Europe has brains. I guess Brussels isn't our city. Maybe we should try Copenhagen."

The four of them drove to Linda's home in the suburbs for the day, and sat on her lawn, soaking up the sun for several hours. They invited her to return to the city with them for dinner, but she had a date. She invited them to stay with her, rather than at the hotel, but Levy decided he didn't want to get her involved any more than she already was. If the police were closing in, he wanted to spare her if he could. "She was a real lady, very respected in Brussels," he says. "She really hadn't done all that much anyway. Why get her mixed up and maybe sent to jail? There wasn't much sense hanging around Brussels if we weren't going to score on the jewelry anyway."

Linda said that as long as they insisted on going back into the city, they should have dinner at her favorite restaurant. It was in the old part of Brussels, she said, but it was magnificent.

"It was even better than that," Levy says. "I've been to all the best restaurants in New York and Paris and Beverly Hills and this was the most gorgeous place I'd ever seen. It was in a square with fountains all around it, and everything looked really well-preserved, even though it was about four hundred years old. The crystal chandeliers looked handmade. So did all the furniture. They prepared the food downstairs and sent it upstairs in a dumbwaiter. It was all very impressive. Of course, taking Tony to a class place like that is like taking a gorilla to the opera. First thing he says is, 'Not a bad-looking dump. Pretty old, though, ain't it?'

"The service was incredible. You put an olive pit in the ashtray and they whisk it away and bring you a new one. We got one wine with the soup and another with the salad and another with the entree and . . . Tony's guzzling the wine and shoveling the food in like there's no tomorrow, but he's not happy with the service. He says it's too slow. He thinks a group of about a dozen Japanese at the table next to us are getting better service. He starts banging his fork against his wine glass. "Hey, how come everything's so slow around here? How come those slant-eyed Japs are getting served before us? Who the hell are they?"

Levy wanted to crawl under the table. In a quiet, intimate room like this one, Bruno's ill-tempered outburst sounded like the roar of a rhino in heat. When the entree came—roast duck, with a choice of orange sauce or brandied sauce with whole cranberries—Levy's mouth began to water. It was, he says, the most delicious-looking dish he'd ever seen. But when the waiter served it, he only cut about three or four slices for each of them. He left most of the meat on the carcass, and when he started to carry the carcass away, Bruno yelped, "Hey, where the hell you going with my duck?" The waiter pointed to his plate: "You have the duck, *monsieur*." Bruno wasn't satisfied: "What the hell are you gonna do with the bones?" The waiter just walked away.

Levy, Bernstein and Bruno finished off their meal with cherries jubilee, cognac and cigars. Then the check came. There had been no prices on the menu, and they had no idea what to expect. With Levy and Bernstein having all but exhausted their limited finances in settling the Paris hotel bill, it was up to Bruno to pay. He took one look at the check—$124 and change—and let out a scream of anguish that was probably heard all the way to Budapest. Mortified, Levy bolted from the table and ran downstairs, into the street. Even outside the restaurant, you could hear Bruno bellowing: "You can charge them dumb Japs these kind of prices if you want, but I'm an American. I'm not that dumb. What do you think I am anyway, a lobster?"

When he was all through insulting the Japanese, the Belgians, the French and every other non-American group he could think of, Bruno paid the bill, and he and Bernstein joined Levy outside for the brief walk back to the hotel.

The next morning, they decided to fly to Copenhagen and try their jewelry ruse there. But when they had originally asked Bruno to make their reservations at the Brussels Hilton, they had done so assuming they could use Bernstein's TWA Getaway card to pay the bill. After their experience at the Paris Hilton, they didn't want to take that chance. Bruno said he'd pay the bill in cash.

"When we came downstairs to check out," Levy says, "there was a big group of Japanese tourists standing in line at the cashier's window. There must have been forty-two of them. Right away, I knew Tony was gonna make trouble. No way he was gonna stand patiently in line while forty-two Japs paid their bills—not after what happened in the restaurant the night before. Leonard and I walked on ahead, toward the jewelry store off the hotel lobby, just to window-shop and get out of the line of fire. All of a sudden, we hear ·Tony's voice· 'Hey, you slant-eyed bastards, get the hell out of my way. I remember December seventh. You guys get away with sneaking in and bombing my country once, and now you think you deserve to eat before me and get taken care of in hotels before me the rest of your lives. Out of my way.' "

Levy was afraid to look back toward the cashier's window, but morbid curiosity riveted his eyes there. What he saw was Bruno shoving the Japanese aside like so many ten-pins in a bowling alley. "Oh, my God," Levy thought. "We're all gonna get thrown in jail for assault and battery, attempted murder and probably rape and genocide to boot." He sprinted toward the front door. But it was a revolving door, and he got his briefcase wedged in it and couldn't get out. Just then, another man tried to walk in the same door. They both got stuck, each trapped in his own glass compartment. After what seemed an eternity, Levy extricated himself and his briefcase from the revolving door and staggered outside. Bernstein wasn't far behind; Bruno—having moved rather quickly to the head of the check-out line—joined them in a matter of minutes.

After an uneventful flight to Copenhagen, the three men checked into the Hotel D'Angleterre. By then, the arrests of four of his partners and the scenes Tony Bruno was making had turned Levy into a virtual basket case. He was absolutely certain his own arrest was imminent. When a man glanced at them a moment too long in the lobby of the D'Angleterre, Levy told Bernstein he was a plainclothes cop. When the desk clerk asked to see their passports, he told Bruno they were obviously on a Denmark wanted list. Ever since they began the jewelry swindle, Levy had been terrified that the *real* Leonard Bernstein, back in New York, might find out what they were doing. "What if Wyersberg calls him, just to verify something?" he kept asking his partners. "Even if they believe us, suppose they want to call us on something and can't find us. Maybe they'll call the New York Philharmonic office. We'll be dead."

The *real* Leonard Bernstein never did hear about what

they were doing—although, ironically, the FBI did go see him a couple of years later when, yet another Leonard Bernstein began masquerading as him on a bad-check spree —but Levy was convinced he would come swooping down on them in Copenhagen any moment, baton in hand. Bruno and Bernstein tried to humor him. Bruno, in particular, kept saying, "Look, Alan, the real Leonard Bernstein is too busy playing big shot to be bothered with what we're doing. Wyersberg thinks we're on our way to Spain, then to Los Angeles, anyway. Why would they call New York? Besides, we're Americans. They're not gonna arrest us in some two-bit country like Denmark."

"Americans?" Levy finally sneered. "These days, that and a quarter won't get you a cup of coffee. This whole thing stinks. I smell it."

The Hotel D'Angleterre was at one end of a shopping mall that connected the hotel with Tivoli Gardens, and as soon as Bruno and Bernstein had Levy somewhat calmed down, they all went for a walk through the mall. They entered the first jewelry store they saw that had no credit card decals on the windows.

"Right away, Leonard picks out a six-foot tall clock," Levy says. "It wasn't even a cuckoo clock, just a big stand-up clock—a grandfather clock, I guess, a big *farkokte* clock with a pendulum."

Levy looked at Bernstein. "Leonard, are you crazy?" I came here for a watch, not a clock." Bernstein said, "Okay, we'll look at watches." They picked out three expensive Piagets, but the salesman said he would have to speak with his boss before he accepted their check for $3,000. The boss, he said, was out just then. Levy tried to persuade him to accept the check himself. No luck. Not even for Leonard Bernstein. "Okay," Levy said, "we'll leave our checks with you, and come back in an hour or so to pick up our watches." When they returned, the salesman said he'd spoken with the boss, and the boss wouldn't accept the checks until he had a chance to verify them with Levy's and Bernstein's banks. The owner had recently sold some jewelry to an American, the salesman said, and the check had bounced. He didn't want to risk being burned again.

For Levy, that was the final straw. If someone else was playing the same game they were, it wouldn't be long before every jewelry store—and every cop—in Europe would catch on. He took the checks back, tore them up and told Bernstein and Bruno he was going home. They walked back to the hotel, and the desk clerk again asked to see their passports. As soon as they were returned—without explanation—the three men left Copenhagen for the United States.

"I figured we'd be arrested the minute we stepped off the plane in Los Angeles," Levy says, "but I was willing to take my medicine. If I was going to be arrested, I wanted to be arrested in the United States. If they caught us in Europe, they might extradite us to Dusseldorf on the jewelry scam and then you could forget about us forever. We'd be in jail in Germany until *yontif* freezes over. I could see the headlines already: 'Two Jews Arrested in Rape at Dachau.'

"Even if we got extradited to London or Zurich or Basel or Luxembourg on the stock scam, I figured they'd put us away for life. In the U.S., I knew what the score was. I knew we'd get bail there. I knew I could find an attorney to get the charges knocked down to something not too bad. Hell, the laws in the U.S. make things a lot easier for a criminal than the laws in any other country. In the U.S., you're innocent until proven guilty. And proving anyone guilty ain't all that easy. In most other countries, all the cops gotta do is have a vague suspicion you might have committed the crime and it's goodbye, off to the dungeon. You gotta prove you're innocent. With no money and a language barrier to boot, I didn't figure to prove my innocence to anybody—especially since I *wasn't* innocent. I wanted to get back to the United States. Fast."

For three men expecting to be met at the airport by the police, the FBI and the gestapo, Levy, Bruno and Bernstein had a remarkably lighthearted flight home. Maybe it was because they had no trouble buying the flight tickets with Bernstein's Pan American Airways credit card. Maybe it was because Bernstein spent most of the flight signing autographs for the other passengers. Maybe, Levy thinks, it was just the relief of knowing that all the running and scheming were over.

When they landed, Bruno and Bernstein cleared Customs easily. But Levy's bags were searched thoroughly—"very thoroughly," he says. "They tore the damn things apart. They were waiting for me, absolutely waiting for me." Fortunately, all the jewelry was in Bruno's suitcase. The three men emerged from Customs and there was no one waiting for them. Levy couldn't believe it. He had been sure they would be arrested before they left the airport; the Customs search had only confirmed that fear. But there were no cops in sight, no FBI agents—"no nothing." Levy and Bernstein reclaimed three of the five pieces of jewelry they had hidden in Bruno's suitcase. They gave him the other two—both watches—as payment of his help, and the three men went their separate ways.

A few days later, the jewelry Bernstein had ordered from Paris arrived in the mail—all $35,230 worth. Levy's jewelry arrived, too—all $15,941 worth. "The goddamn mailman just left it on my front lawn," Levy says. "It wasn't insured. There was no mention of duty. He just dumped a box with fifteen thousand dollars' worth of jewelry on my lawn."

Levy and Bernstein mailed their checks to Wyersberg, and then—on July 13—telephoned the store to order more jewelry.

"Leonard told the guy we'd received our jewelry in the mail and we were so pleased with it, we wanted to do some early Christmas shopping," Levy says. "The guy was only too happy to oblige. Leonard ordered about thirty-five thousand dollars' worth of jewelry. He just gave the guy a general idea of what he wanted and told him to pick out the specific pieces. I ordered about fifteen thousand dollars' worth and did the same thing."

Less than a week later, they called Wyersberg again and ordered even more jewelry.

"We'd given them our first checks on July second," Levy says. "According to what we'd been told, they wouldn't know the checks were no good until July twenty-eighth. We made our last order July twenty-first."

With $65,000 worth of jewelry in hand and even more than that on the way, Levy and Bernstein set about insuring and disposing of their treasure. They went to the prestigious Marvin Hime Company of Beverly Hills—right down the street from Martin Calaway's office—to have some of the jewelry appraised. Hime appraised the jewelry at less than the price which Wyersberg had charged. Still, Hime appraised eight pieces at $32,000. They went to the Like and Nash Insurance Agency to have those eight pieces and the rest of the jewelry insured. "No sense taking any chances," Levy says. "Now that we were back in the States, we figured we were practically the legitimate owners of the jewelry. We'd been told they'd never get us for writing bad checks in Europe if we got back here safely."

Armed with his appraisal and his insurance, Levy tried to sell the jewelry. He talked to bookies, hoods, friends, former business associates. No one was interested. Then he and Bernstein received letters from the United States Customs office informing them that their July 13 order had arrived. The packages could not be released, however, until they paid $2,700 in duty. They didn't have $2,700.

"We took three of the best pieces and hopped a plane to Vegas," Levy says. "I figured we could sell the stuff to a couple of guys I knew there, and raise the dough to get the rest of the stuff from Customs." Again, no sale. They returned to Los Angeles, took eight pieces to the Hollywood

Collateral Loan Company, and pawned them for $7,500. That would more than cover the duty, they figured, and as soon as they were able to start selling the other jewelry, they'd reclaim the eight pieces. They bought certified checks totalling $2,700 and went to claim their jewelry from Customs.

"I noticed the seal on one of Leonard's packages seemed to be open," Levy says. "I told the guy I wasn't giving him any money until I checked inside and made sure the jewelry was there. For all I knew, it might have been stolen or damaged."

The Customs officer said he would open the package. He did. It was empty. He opened another. It was empty, too.

"They were all empty," Levy says. "Fifteen or twenty boxes for Leonard and ten or fifteen for me—all empty. It was pretty obvious what had happened. Either Wyersberg had caught on and sent the empty boxes deliberately, or the FBI emptied them. We never did find out which, but either way, it was a trap. They wanted us to pay the duty and sign the receipt for the jewelry. Then they could use that evidence against us. For all we knew, the cops were probably waiting right there, hiding until we signed the receipts."

Levy grabbed Bernstein by the wrist: "Let's get out of here." But Bernstein wasn't giving up that easily. "I want to see the inspector," he demanded. "I want to see the postmaster general. I want to see the FBI. Someone's stolen my jewelry."

Levy tried to drag him away.

"Alan, we've been fucked," Bernstein shrieked.

"We've been fucked?" Levy countered, incredulously. "Come on, let's get out of here before something worse happens. The FBI probably has our jewelry already."

"They can't do that," Bernstein said. "That's stealing. That's tampering with the United States mails. That's against the law."

Bernstein insisted on filing a report with the Customs office, listing the missing merchandise as stolen.

A few days later, he got a letter from the German consul in Los Angeles. The first check had bounced. The consul wanted to talk to him about the jewelry. Levy called the consul and identified himself as Bernstein. The consul politely suggested he come by the consulate.

"If you want to talk to me," Levy said, "I'll be glad to talk. But not in your consulate. Meet me at Nibbler's in Beverly Hills or somewhere like that. I'm not coming down to your consulate. You're not putting me in a Mercedes and on a Lufthansa jet back to Germany. Sorry. No way."

The next thing Levy knew, there was a police captain from Dusseldorf in Los Angeles, looking for him and Bernstein. Levy went to see the attorney who had told him not to worry about passing bad checks in Dusseldorf. "Are you sure we won't be prosecuted?" he asked. The attorney said he was. He called his friend in the district attorney's office again to confirm his opinion. The deputy district attorney said he was right. Levy decided he had nothing to worry about on the jewelry scam. Wyersberg had probably sent the empty boxes just to scare him. The letter from the German consulate and the presence of the detective from Dusseldorf were probably part of the same strategy. They knew they had no legal hold on him, but they were hoping to frighten him into making at least a partial payment. "Screw 'em!" Levy decided. "I got enough to worry about on the stock. I know I'm gonna get arrested on that any day."

He wanted to check with Ralph Ernsten and Bo Farmer and a few of his other partners, but he was afraid they were being followed and all their telephones were tapped by now. He decided to sit tight for a while.

During this time, Levy and his wife and daughter moved from their home in Cheviot Hills to an apartment in Westwood, a couple of blocks from where Tony Bruno lived. Levy had never felt comfortable in the Cheviot Hills home for some reason, and with the law closing in, he felt even less comfortable. He wanted to spend his final days of freedom in more pleasant surroundings.

At eight o'clock on the morning of August 4, there was a sharp knock on the front door of Levy's new apartment. He answered the door with his little girl in his arms. It was the FBI—two agents. They said they wanted to talk to him about "some stock from the Jeffries Banknote Company."

"I have nothing to say," he told them.

They asked if they could come in for a few minutes.

"I have nothing to say."

Levy had been expecting this moment for weeks now, and he was surprisingly calm. But when the FBI agents asked him, "Don't you want to help your country? Aren't you a patriotic citizen? This matter involves people from foreign countries." Levy burst into laughter. "Who am I all of a sudden—George Washington?" he asked. The FBI agents said they would see him later. Levy slammed the door in their faces.

The next day, the FBI went to see Bernstein. A few days later, Tony Bruno was arrested while trying to burglarize a house. While he was in custody, someone burglarized *his* house—and took the watches he'd gotten from Levy and Bernstein.

"The whole fucking world was falling apart," Levy says. "It was the worst period of my whole life. It was like I was already dead. I figured they knew all about the stock, and any minute I was going to jail. I was like a condemned man on death row. Even Frannie had pretty well figured out what was going on by this time. That didn't make things any better."

Early on the morning of August 17—almost seven months after his first meeting with Steve Berg and Gerry Kassap in East Los Angeles—Alan Levy was arrested.

Chapter 9

As soon as the door bell rang, I knew it was the FBI. Nobody else comes to my house at eight o'clock in the morning. Their office was just down the street from me, so I guess they decided to pick me up on the way to work."

Levy, resigned to his fate by then, went along quietly.

"It was the same two FBI guys as the first time. When I answered the door, one of them said, 'We have a warrant for your arrest from the United States Attorney's office.' I just put my hands out to be handcuffed. But they were very nice. Frannie and the baby were there, and one of the FBI guys said, 'No, not here, not in front of the little girl.' When I asked if I could get dressed, they said, 'Sure, go ahead.' They even took me out the back door of the apartment building so none of the neighbors would see me. 'We don't want to embarrass you,' they told me."

On the ride downtown, Levy asked the FBI agents what his bail would be. One of the agents said, "I don't know, Alan—probably pretty high. You got plenty of money." Levy realized they were trying to be friendly, hoping to pump him for information. He decided to play along.

"That's right. I got plenty— in Switzerland."

The FBI agent nodded. "Yes. we know."

"I got a million bucks. Tell you what. Let me go and we'll split it three ways."

"Okay. Where is it?"

"Just pull over and let me out."

"Huh?"

"Let me out. I'll go get it and send you your share by check."

Both FBI agents broke into laughter.

The rest of the ride downtown was uneventful, but when Levy got to the courthouse, Bernstein was already there. Levy wondered where everyone else was—Ralph Ernsten and Bo Farmer and Steve Berg and Gordon Iler and all his other partners in the stock swindle. He also wondered where his attorney was. He called Frannie and asked her to have him arrange for bail.

When they were brought before the magistrate, the magistrate read the charges against them: Interstate transportation of stolen or fraudulently obtained jewelry.

"Jewelry?" Levy yelped. He had assumed he and Bernstein had been arrested on the stock swindle; he thought he was home free on the jewelry. Only later did he learn that the assurances he had been given that he wouldn't be prosecuted for passing bad checks in Europe had been incorrect. The policy was not to prosecute bad checks passed in Europe *only* if the checks were for less than $5,000. Levy's first check had been within that limit—$3,361. If he had quit there, he would probably have escaped prosecution. But he had sent a second check—for $15,941—when the first shipment of jewelry arrived in Los Angeles. That had been his undoing.

Bail was set at $10,000 each for Levy and Bernstein, and—with his attorney still not in court—Levy called Frannie and arranged to have his cousin pay the $1,000 necessary to secure a $10,000 bail bond.

The next day, Levy went to see his old bookie/friend, "Marty the Nose." Marty, he figured, could recommend a good attorney. Levy didn't want to have anything more to do with his old attorney: "That son-of-a-bitch told me I didn't have anything to worry about on the jewelry scam; then, when I got arrested, he didn't even show up to bail me out."

Marty suggested Levy see Michael Nasatir, a bright, idealistic young attorney who had once worked for the U.S. Attorney's office and was now in private practice. Nasatir had an excellent reputation in the federal courts, Marty said. Levy liked the idea immediately. He had met Nasatir back when Nasatir was in law school, dating a young woman who managed one of Levy's ready-to-wear stores— the same woman who ultimately married Steve Berg.

Levy went to see Nasatir and his partner Victor Sherman. They agreed to take the case. Bernstein, meanwhile, hired another attorney.

"Michael was an absolutely marvelous attorney—and an even better friend," Levy says. "I told him my whole story, and right from the beginning, he told me to tell the truth. He said he'd rather plead me guilty, if he had to, than have me perjure myself. He gave me an hour-and-a-half lecture the first time, and when he was through, I knew I was in the right hands. I knew he was good, and I knew he genuinely cared about me."

From what Nasatir could find out, it didn't seem that the authorities had an airtight case against Levy yet on the jewelry scam. They had probably arrested him prematurely, he decided, just to let Levy know they were on to him. That would probably stop him from continuing with either the stock or jewelry swindle while they finished their investigations. Cut off from the funds in those operations, he wasn't likely to run away and hide.

"But that didn't really bother me," Levy says. "I wasn't planning to go anywhere anyway. Once they got me, they got me. I was just going to tell them everything and hope for the best."

Investigation and interrogation in the stock and jewelry cases dragged on for almost six months before Grand Jury indictments were returned. At one time or another, there were four different U.S. Attorneys prosecuting the case— one of whom was killed in a Hollywood love triangle. All the while, Levy was living in limbo. He had no more stock left: Tony Bruno had burned the stock Davidson had; the police in Europe had the stock Levy had given to Shinwell and Tom Wilson; the FBI in Los Angeles had the stock in Kassap's plant. Levy didn't even have any of the jewelry left. His share had been pawned to raise the money to pay duty on what had turned out to be empty boxes, and the FBI had taken Bernstein's jewelry back. With the police and FBI visiting him almost as regularly as his own attorney, Levy couldn't very well start a new swindle. But with the threat of a long prison sentence hanging over his head, he couldn't rouse himself to seek out a legitimate business enterprise either.

"I'd just get it going and I'd be sent to the joint," he says. "Why bother?"

Reluctantly, Levy reactivated his sports forecasting service. He had first started the service in the spring of 1970 at the suggestion of an old friend from Chicago. Levy's friend had known a sports tout in Houston who advised bettors on football and basketball, but wasn't interested in baseball. Levy and his friend considered themselves experts on all sports, including baseball, and they had persuaded the Houston tout to sell them his client list so they could set up their own tip service for baseball. They soon expanded to football and basketball, too, but Levy always lost more money on his own bets than he made selling advice to other bettors. After an initial success, the sports forecasting service had floundered. But now, with nothing better to do and time hanging heavy on his hands, Levy started sending out his sports tout sheet again. He also resumed betting heavily himself. In a single weekend, he lost what little money he had left from his share of the

$7,500 he had gotten when he pawned the jewelry. Then his luck changed. He won more than $5,000 the next weekend. But before he could spend it—or even savor it—he received a call from his attorney. To no one's surprise, the authorities were insisting that Levy and Bernstein make complete restitution to the Wyersberg Jewelry Company on the jewelry they had swindled. That meant they would have to come up with $7,500 to reclaim the jewelry they had pawned. Levy called Bernstein. All Bernstein could come up with, he said, was $1,500. The authorities wanted the restitution made quickly, as a preliminary condition of plea negotiations with Levy and Bernstein. Grudgingly, Levy gave his attorney $6,000 to pay for his share and help Bernstein pay his.

Nasatir turned the money over to the authorities, and they reclaimed the jewelry and returned it to Wyersberg in Dusseldorf.

"I was pissed," Levy says, "but I really just wanted to get the whole thing over and done with as fast as possible. If that meant paying part of Leonard's share, fuck it, I'd pay."

Nothing Levy touched during the time he was awaiting trial seemed to turn out right. He even tried to help a few friends bail out troubled businesses, and all failed miserably. Then he and his Chicago friend got involved in the import of German bicycles. The two of them were to have the exclusive United States distributorship for the company. But that, too, fell apart. His friend invested $100,-000 in the venture and lost almost half his money. Levy felt responsible. About the same time, Levy's wife, Frannie, left him. "She just got tired of living the way we were living," he says. "I don't really blame her. We had kind of a marginal existence, with me about to go to jail for God knows how long. For most of our marriage, I'd been scamming and scheming and betting. I was always good to the baby, but it really wasn't much of a life for Frannie."

Levy wanted to keep his daughter with him, but he

knew neither Frannie nor the courts would permit that. Still, Nicole became his whole life. He would call her several times a day, try to see her at least once a day, take her with him on weekends. He badgered Frannie incessantly about Nicole—"Make sure she drinks her milk." "Did she wear her coat to school this morning?" "Did you watch her take her vitamins?" When Nicole was sick, even with a mild cold, Levy practically lived on the telephone, demanding hourly reports on her temperature and eating and bowel habits.

Not having Nicole with him all the time only deepened Levy's depression. One day, disconsolate, he went to his attorney for advice. Nasatir suggested he see a psychiatrist. "Mike said it would probably help me understand myself better," Levy says. "He also said it would look good on a probation report when we finally went to trial; it would look like I knew I'd done something wrong and was trying to get help and do something to rehabilitate myself."

Levy went to the psychiatrist for about eight months. He started with three sessions a week, then cut back to two, then one. At $35 each, he couldn't afford to go as often as the psychiatrist wanted to see him. But even on a limited, weekly basis, Levy benefitted from the psychiatric treatment.

"I can't really say it changed me," he says, "but at least, it helped me to understand why I do the things I do. I came to realize that my gambling wasn't so much a sickness the way it is with some people; it's really just a way of getting excitement and attention and looking important. The psychiatrist also helped me see a lot of things about my relationships with women and other people, especially my daughter. He said the reason I was so devoted to her was because I was looking for the kind of undying, unquestioning love from her that I never got from my mother or any of my wives. My folks were divorced when I was five or six, and I had to live with my aunt and my

THE LEVY CAPER 187

grandparents. I didn't live with my mother again until I was about eleven, up in Canada. The psychiatrist said I never had the kind of love a child has to have from his mother. All my marriages were a little strange, too. My second wife left me for one of her wealthy boy friends. My third wife, Rocky, was seven years older than me—a nymphomaniac who paid me twenty-five thousand dollars to marry her, then went to bed with another guy while I was down in Tijuana betting on the dog races a few days after we got married. I even married one woman twice. But she left me both times. They all left me really. The psychiatrist told me I knew I could always count on my little girl, Nicole, to love me. She could never leave me like my mother and my wives had. You can't get a divorce from your father. I would always be her father. She would always love me."

But the psychiatrist never did make Levy feel guilty about what he had done with the stock or the jewelry. Just the opposite.

"I was starting to feel guilty when I was arrested," he says. "I was really down. I thought I was a detriment to society. The psychiatrist showed me that just wasn't so."

Levy came away from his psychiatric treatment convinced that he merely exploited the greed of others.

"I never hurt anyone physically, and I couldn't hurt anyone financially if they weren't so greedy," he says. "You can't con an honest man. You can only con someone who's looking for something for nothing, trying to get a little under the table. Banks make loans they shouldn't make just so they can collect the interest. Stores take checks and credit cards without checking them because they're afraid they'll lose too many sales otherwise. Credit card companies give cards to obviously poor credit risks because they're greedy for that three percent or five percent service charge and all that monthly interest. Everyone's looking for the quick buck, the easy buck. The only difference between me and the so-called legitimate businessman is that I admit I'm a thief. I tell you up front I'm going to drill you a new asshole. They pretend they're respectable pillars of society, but they're stashing dough away in their pockets and safe deposit boxes and Swiss bank accounts. They just do it in a socially acceptable way. That's the hypocrisy of our society. Our society says it's okay to artificially inflate the prices of some goods and get rich off it, but it's not okay to be a con man who tells the world up front that he's a con man."

At first, Levy didn't want to cooperate with the authorities investigating the stock and jewelry cases. Nor was his attorney sure he should cooperate. "There were some jurisdictional questions involved," Nasatir says. "No one could really prove that Alan ever actually transported the stock across state lines or out of the country. We considered fighting the case, but with both the stock and the jewelry hanging over him we were just afraid they'd nail him on at least one case and send him away for a long time."

Even so, Levy's own peculiar code of ethics wouldn't permit him to squeal on his partners. It was only when they all began squealing on him—and denying their own roles in the crime—that he agreed to talk to authorities himself. Almost everyone involved in the case was willing to talk, so the FBI had no shortage of information. But few stories jibed. Everyone except Levy was busy trying to protect himself and shading the truth toward that end. The FBI was questioning everyone—Levy, Steve Berg, Gerry Kassap, Bo Farmer, John Dubeck, Gordon Iler, everyone—but the inconsistencies among many of the stories, combined with the sheer volume and complexity of the stock manipulations, delayed completion of the investigation. Nasatir had good sources in the case, so he knew when the other suspects were talking and what they were saying. Then, over dinner with several attorneys one night, Nasatir heard that one of the conspirators, Fred Ryan, had agreed to testify before the Grand Jury. Nasatir decided it was time for Levy to tell everything.

"The only thing we really had to bargain with was that Alan was the only guy who knew the whole story, from beginning to end," Nasatir says. "Fortunately, I heard enough from the U.S. Attorney's office to know that what most of the others were saying was bullshit. I also had enough truth in the bank with the U.S. Attorney that they would at least listen to me and check out what I and Alan said. They were pretty dubious about what they were hearing from everyone else anyway. The one thing I really had to convince them of—my top priority—was that Alan just wasn't a master criminal."

On February 1, 1972, a federal Grand Jury in Los Angeles indicted Levy in the stock case. The official charge was conspiracy to transport stolen securities across state lines. Among those indicted with him were Gerald Kassap, Mario Denard, Ernest Shinwell, Gordon Iler, Bo Farmer, Robert Cox and H. Cabot Jones. Subsequent indictments named most of the others involved in the abortive swindle. But Levy, the authorities were still convinced, was the central figure, the mastermind. FBI investigators spoke of him as a sophisticated international swindler with vast underworld connections. One FBI agent even warned that he could have been a threat to the Free World economy. If his $800 million worth of stock had fallen into Communist hands, they said, several major American companies might have been plunged into bankruptcy by unscrupulous stock manipulation.

The United States Attorney's office felt the same way about Levy. They wanted to prosecute him to the fullest extent of their capabilities. They wanted him given the maximum sentence—five years in prison and a $10,000 fine —on each count in the case. But that strategy was based on the assumption that Levy was, indeed, a sophisticated underworld swindler with vast underworld connections—a

hopelessly incorrigible sociopath. As the investigation continued, however, it became clear that Levy just wasn't the
master criminal everyone made him out to be. It also became clear that his winning personality and his willingness
to tell the truth about the case just might save him from a
long prison sentence. Levy is so compulsively honest about
his compulsive dishonesty, so utterly charming in his
roguery, that it is virtually impossible to dislike him once
you've spent more than ten minutes with him—even if you're
a prosecuting attorney whose job it is to put him in jail.
Moreover, of the more than thirty people involved in the
stock swindle, Levy was the only one who consistently told
authorities the truth about his own role in the case; all the
other witnesses and defendants tried to color the story to
minimize their roles and make themselves appear to have
been either innocent bystanders or ignorant pawns.

"All the other suspects tried to make Alan the fall-guy,"
says one investigator. "They said they thought the stock
was legitimate or they didn't understand what they were
doing. We knew that was bullshit, and every time we
checked out something Alan told us, he was right."

At one point in pre-trial negotiations, it looked as if Levy
might be lying. Orange County authorities said they could
prove that Levy had pocketed all $65,000 from the two
loans Finn Konsmo made at the bank there. If that were
true, they said, they would see to it that Levy got the
maximum sentence in Orange County, regardless of what
deal he might be able to work out with authorities in Los
Angeles County. That frightened Levy. There were three
separate cases against him—the stock swindle in Los Angeles
County, the stock swindle and bank loan in Orange County
and the jewelry scam. If he got the maximum sentence on
each, he could face a fifteen-year prison term and a $30,-
000 fine. Even if he were able to negotiate minimum sentences on the jewelry scam and the stock swindle within
Los Angeles' jurisdiction, he might still face a five-year
prison term in Orange County.

Fortunately for Levy, all the payments from the two Orange County loans had been made by check—except for the $5,000 he had insisted on in cash. It was a simple matter to subpoena the checks from the bank files and prove they had neither been made payable to Levy nor endorsed by him. But all the other suspects in the case still insisted Levy was responsible for everything. He, clearly, was going to be their scapegoat. The authorities in Orange County weren't sure what to do. Finally, they decided to threaten Levy with vigorous prosecution if he didn't tell them everything he knew. He agreed—on one condition:

"I gotta have immunity. You gotta give me a guarantee of immunity—in writing. I don't want to stand trial in Orange County."

Levy was absolutely inflexible on that point. He knew Orange County's reputation as a conservative, law-and-order county—one of the few big urban areas outside the Deep South, for example, that had voted for Barry Goldwater for President in 1964. The District Attorney in Orange County is a man named Cecil Hicks, one of the most effective and resourceful prosecutors in the state when he was a trial attorney, and now a man with a reputation as a no-nonsense administrator. Hicks is not actually the hard-line conservative many think him to be—though he is essentially conservative—and he and Levy, ironically, have quite a bit in common. Philosophically, Levy is just as much a law-and-order man—and just as much a political conservative—as Hicks is, for example. And both men are witty raconteurs, both take their football seriously, both are attractive to women (despite being unusually short), both are immensely likable—garrulous extroverts who are great fun to be around, in an office or at a party. Like Levy, Hicks is something of an imp—"a perennial Peck's bad boy, Andy Hardy goes to court and gives the judge a hotfoot," a newspaper reporter once wrote of him; "a freckle-faced kid [who] ought to be wearing tennis shoes and patched Levis, with a bag of marbles sticking out of his pocket," the police chief in a neighboring city once said of him.

But Levy wanted no part of Hicks or an Orange County judge and jury.

"It would be bad there for anyone," he says. "For a Jew? Forget it. I wanted no part of that. They'd hang me by my toenails."

Orange County authorities agreed to grant Levy immunity only if he passed a lie detector test. That, he said, was fine. But he flunked the lie detector test.

"I told them the truth, except for one thing I left out," he says. "I 'forgot' to mention Steve Berg's name. He was no criminal. I tried to protect him everyplace, but especially in Orange County. I figured a jury there would do the same thing to a guy named Berg that they would to a guy named Levy."

Although Levy flunked the Orange County lie detector test, authorities there decided to give him immunity anyway. They were convinced that he was telling the truth—or most of the truth—their own scientific examinations notwithstanding. They believed him because much of what he said confirmed what they had learned from their independent investigations. Levy, for example, implicated the banker who made the loan to Finn Konsmo. Konsmo and everyone else had tried to protect the banker. But Orange County authorities had been suspicious of the banker for some time, and what Levy said coincided with what they had learned in a preliminary inquiry. Levy also benefited from a friendship between his attorney and the first Orange County prosecutor to handle the case. The prosecutor, like the U.S. Attorney's office in Los Angeles, was at least willing to listen to Levy because he knew and trusted Nasatir. Levy's cooperation in Los Angeles stood him in further good stead in Orange County. The U.S. Attorney's office made sure that Orange County authorities knew he had cooperated and that they had believed his story. In fact,

their agreement to pass that information along to the Orange
County District Attorney's office was part of the bargain
Levy's attorney made for his complete cooperation in Los
Angeles.

All these factors became incidental, though, once authorities spoke with Levy and saw him for what he was.

"As the FBI and all the cops and prosecutors got further
into the case, they realized I just wasn't a master criminal,
no matter what all my co-conspirators said," Levy says.
"How could any sophisticated swindler do as many stupid
things as I'd done and get taken by as many of my partners as I'd been taken by? If I was a sophisticated swindler,
then Joe Namath was a Sicilian monk. The FBI would
see my fingerprints all over the stock and they'd just laugh.
I'd tell them about using the paper bags to carry the stock
around in and they'd just shake their heads. We'd talk
about how Shinwell put me away and they'd just know I
was no genius of the underworld. I mean Shinwell, it turns
out, was no Little Lord Fauntleroy after all. He was a real
bad-ass. He had good contacts with the Mafia here—and I
mean good contacts."

Shinwell, federal authorities told Levy, was one of the
smoothest and most notorious con-men in the English-
speaking world. He virtually made his living dealing in
stolen securities and other fradulent schemes. Though most
of the details of his machinations would not become public
knowledge until the fall of 1973, when Senator Henry Jackson's Permanent Subcommittee on Investigations would hold
hearings in Washington, the FBI already had a thick dossier
on him.

As a witness before Sen. Jackson's subcommittee would
later testify, Shinwell had approached him and others with
a scheme remarkably similar to Levy's in December 1970.
Like Levy, Shinwell had millions of dollars' worth of stock
in major American companies, and he wanted to place it
with banks as collateral for large loans. Like Levy, he didn't

own the stock. It was, the witness said, stolen. But Shinwell, being a professional at that sort of thing, didn't make the same amateurish mistake Levy would make with his partners. He had told his prospective customer the stock was legitimate.

Other witnesses before Senator Jackson's subcommittee would tie Shinwell to a massive international investment fraud using $10 million in "phony letters of credit," foreign and domestic banks and several organized crime figures "to reap huge illegal profits." Among the mobsters linked to the scheme were Jasper Joseph "Fats" Aiello, "an associate of members of the Cleveland mob"; Sebastian "Buster" Aloi, "organized crime boss of south Florida"; Johnny "Sideburns" Cerella, "a front man . . . for a captain of the late Vito Genovese family"; and Angelo Bruno, "crime boss of Philadelphia."

As Levy said when the FBI told him about all this, "No wonder Shinwell was never scared when I talked about going back to my 'associates' in the States to get some muscle. He was probably laughing at me under his breath."

Shinwell wasn't the only one of his "partners" whose background proved a surprise to Levy. In the course of the investigation, he became sufficiently friendly with his prosecutors to learn some of the inside secrets of the case against him. The most stunning of these was that there was no Mr. Todd, the mysterious friend of Ralph Ernsten who supposedly had Swiss banking connections and could quickly convert $5 million worth of stock to $3 million in spendable cash.

Ernsten was an FBI informer. "Mr. Todd" was his contact in the FBI. When Ernsten had called "Mr. Todd" from that meeting in Brentwood, way back in May 1971 when Levy was just getting started with the stock swindle, he was actually talking directly to the FBI. He subsequently delivered the $5 million worth of stock to them personally.

Ernsten had a criminal record five pages long, dating

back to his first arrest on a forgery charge in Duluth, Minnesota, in 1945. He'd been arrested more than a dozen times in Minnesota alone over the years, and he also had been arrested—on a variety of charges—in Oklahoma, Pennsylvania, Iowa, Illinois, Nebraska, Tennessee, Missouri and California. The FBI wouldn't tell Levy how long they had been using Ernsten as an informant, though, because he had—in the words of one federal official—"embarrassed the Bureau," by his behavior in the stock swindle. In a move wholly consistent with the amateur bungling and selfish double-dealing so characteristic of the entire swindle, Ernsten had not kept the FBI informed of all the subsequent deals he and Levy and their partners made. He tipped them off on one deal, then apparently assumed he could get rich on other deals, without their being any the wiser. It was, said the U.S. Attorney, "a classic example of the double-cross"; Ernsten had double-crossed his partners by going to the FBI, then double-crossed the FBI by continuing to make deals with his partners. Ernsten's presence on the inside of the conspiracy and his feeding of information to the FBI, through "Mr. Todd," made the FBI investigation considerably easier than it might otherwise have been. Thanks to Ernsten—and the willingness of the other suspects to talk—the FBI's job was essentially one of assembling a jigsaw puzzle in which they had all the pieces. But Ernsten's double-dealing also helped confuse the FBI at times and temporarily stalled their investigation. They didn't know quite what to make of Ernsten's role in the whole affair.

"The FBI," Levy realized, "had known what we were doing from the very beginning. We were doomed to failure before we even really got started, only none of us knew it—none of us except Ralph, and he was too stupid and too greedy to get out while he could."

The dawning realization that Levy was just a zealous amateur who overstepped the limits of his knowledge prompted authorities to consider going easy on him. But it was his disarming nature—his sheer likability—that helped him the most. He'd sit swapping stories with his prosecutors and investigators, and in time, they grew to look on him as—well, almost as a friend. When Levy first began talking to authorities, he hoped to get off with no jail time. It quickly became clear that that was unacceptable to the prosecution. But a compromise was finally reached: Levy would cooperate fully with the investigation, testify for the prosecution, plead guilty and serve—at most—a six-month sentence. Then the assistant U.S. Attorney who struck that bargain was replaced. The new assistant U.S. Attorney was Richard Kirschner, a brilliant young prosecutor. Kirschner was twenty-eight then, and he'd spent only three years with the U.S. Attorney's office. Within two years, Kirschner would leave the government to open his own practice in Los Angeles, but in 1972, he was a rising star in the Justice Department. Already he had been appointed special prosecutor for the Southern District of Florida in the government's wide-ranging investigation of the Bank of Sark/Trans-Continental Insurance Company mail fraud case, the largest such case in American history. The fraud, run from the Isle of Guernsey off the coast of England, had bilked unsuspecting investors out of $150 million. Kirschner's prosecution had resulted in twenty-two Grand Jury indictments. He was asked to see if he could achieve equally dramatic results in Levy's case. Immediately, Kirschner instituted around-the-clock interrogations, sought search warrants and started hauling in every witness he could find.

When Kirschner learned that his predecessor had promised Levy no more than six months in jail, he exploded. "You gave away the goddamn store," he complained. "Levy's the guy who made this whole thing go—damn near a billion-dollar swindle. How can you let a guy like that off with just six months?"

But by the time Kirschner had finished his investigation,

he, too, found Levy irresistible. He made Levy no promises of leniency, but he did persuade Levy it would be in his best interest to cooperate entirely with the prosecution—even to the extent of being the state's star witness at the trial of Levy's conspirators.

As it turned out, almost all the defendants plea-bargained for relatively light sentences by agreeing to plead guilty to one or two counts—and tell the prosecution all they knew about the case—in exchange for the government's dropping some of the other charges against them. Levy pleaded guilty. Steve Berg pleaded guilty. Gerry Kassap pleaded guilty. Cabot Jones pleaded guilty. Bo Farmer pleaded guilty. Keith Simpson pleaded guilty. John Dubeck pleaded guilty. The list goes on and on. In the cases being prosecuted in Los Angeles, only three men—Ralph Ernsten, Gordon Iler and Bob Cox—refused to plead guilty.

Their trial began in the United States District Courthouse in Los Angeles on January 10, 1973. One by one, the government called its witnesses. Officials of the International Chemical and Nuclear Corporation testified on the origin of the stock certificates. Officials of Chase Manhattan Bank explained their function as transfer agents for the stock. Officials of Jeffries Banknote Company and Certified Incinerator Company traced the route of the stock from New York, through their hands, to the Kassap Rag Company. Then the government began calling the defendants who had already pleaded guilty. Fred Ryan implicated Cox, Iler and Ernsten. So did Farmer. But Dubeck was the critical witness. Cox, Iler and Ernsten hadn't expected him to turn state's evidence. They thought he would be as unyielding as they had been. Instead, he made an excellent witness for the prosecution—calm, precise, sure of himself, neither vengeful nor self-pitying. The prosecutor led Dubeck step-by-step through every element of the stock swindle he had been familiar with, implicating Cox, Iler and

Ernsten more with each answer he gave. Dubeck told the jury all about the meetings with them in the 9000 Club, about his flights to Phoenix and Las Vegas, about payoffs and negotiations and threats and telephone calls.

Within a week after the trial began—and especially after Dubeck's testimony—it became clear to the three defendants that they had no hope of escaping conviction. Levy was to be the final witness—confirming and bringing together everything the other witnesses had said. But Levy never took the stand. Several days before he was to testify, Cox pleaded guilty. The day before he was to testify, Iler and Ernsten pleaded guilty.

Two weeks later, on February 1, Levy appeared before Judge William Gray for sentencing on the stock swindle. When Judge Gray called both the prosecution and defense attorneys into his chambers before passing formal sentence, Richard Kirschner went out of his way to tell the judge how cooperative Levy had been. His sentence: thirty days.

Levy was relieved, but he still had to be sentenced on the jewelry case. That scared him. Judge Gray, he knew, had a reputation for leniency. Judge Matt Byrne, who would sentence him on the jewelry case, was just the opposite. He was a former U.S. Attorney, and he tended to think like a prosecutor. He was not unreasonable, but he was tough. Nasatir tried to see Byrne in chambers. Byrne had been his boss in the U.S. Attorney's office, and he thought Byrne might at least listen to what he had to say about Levy. Byrne refused to see him. He also refused to see Kirschner. Levy wanted both men to try again, but everyone was wary of irritating Byrne. The judge was just then in the midst of the Pentagon Papers trial and the controversy over President Nixon having sent John Ehrlichman to offer him the FBI directorship. It wasn't an especially opportune time to try Matt Byrne's patience. Nasatir decided to make no further attempt to see Byrne, and to hope for the best.

Levy was supposed to be sentenced in the jewelry case the same day he was sentenced on the stock swindle, but Judge Byrne postponed sentencing until the next day. There had been delays and postponements throughout the case, and Levy was getting edgy. He knew he'd have to go to jail eventually, and he wanted to get it over with. He was hoping Byrne wouldn't sentence him to more than thirty days, to run concurrently with Judge Gray's sentence in the stock case. Then his attorney heard that his probation report wasn't particularly good. That, combined with Judge Byrne's refusal to see him in chambers, convinced Nasatir his client was in trouble. "You might get three years," he told Levy.

When they finally got to court for sentencing, the court-room was packed with attorneys, defendants and spectators for the Pentagon Papers trial. Levy was to be sentenced just before the trial resumed after its lunch recess. Levy was already apprehensive over his attorney's warning that he could face a three-year prison sentence. The large crowd further discomfited—and embarrassed —him.

When Byrne called Levy's case, Nasatir made a strong plea for leniency—so strong that Byrne, studying the pro-bation report and Levy's past record, asked if he and Nasa-tir were talking about the same man. At long last, Byrne asked, "Is the defendant ready for sentencing?" Levy nodded. Byrne pronounced sentence:

"Three years . . ."

Levy's knees buckled. He gasped for breath. It seemed, he recalls, like an eternity before Byrne finished:

". . . suspended to ninety days, with five years probation."

Levy's spirits soared. He asked Nasatir if the ninety days would be in addition to the thirty days for the jewelry scam or if they could run concurrently. The judge agreed to run them concurrently. On the way out of the courtroom, Nasatir apologized to Levy. He had always hoped, he said, to keep Levy out of jail altogether—to get a suspended sentence. Levy looked at him as if he were crazy. "We stole the courthouse, Michael. I got a total of only ninety days for a big jewelry scam and an eight-hundred-million-dollar stock swindle, and you're apologizing? C'mon, let's get outta here before they change their minds."

Leonard Bernstein was also sentenced to ninety days on the jewelry scam. Most of the defendants in the stock case got even lighter sentences—generally suspended sentences and two or three years probation. Ralph Ernsten jumped bail, and is still a fugitive. Two other defendants, John Davidson and Mario Denard, are also fugitives. Ernsten also jumped bail in Orange County, where Kassap and Finn Konsmo both pleaded guilty and received light sentences. The judge there dismissed the charges against Konsmo's banker/friend, and the jury acquitted Cabot Jones and Martin Calaway, despite Levy's strong testimony against them.

"The jury was just reluctant to believe that two distinguished-looking men like that would get involved in such a shady deal," said the prosecutor who tried the case. But Jones pleaded guilty in the Los Angeles stock swindle prosecution and was given a suspended sentence and two years probation, and Calaway was subsequently indicted by a federal grand jury in Los Angeles in an unrelated gambling case, in which he was accused of helping to run rigged blackjack and crap games that earned as much as $250,000 a month profit. Investigators said Calaway and six co-defendants—including Peter John Milano, identified by the FBI as a ranking member of the La Cosa Nostra family of Nick Licata—used attractive prostitutes to lure customers into their games. Ironically, one of the key witnesses in that case was none other than John Dubeck. But Dubeck, whose testimony had proved so valuable in the stock swindle trial in Los Angeles, was never permitted to testify in the gambling trial. One week before he was to tell the jury all he knew, he was murdered. Dubeck was a shift manager at the

Westward Ho Casino in Las Vegas by then, and shortly before midnight, Tuesday, March 20, on his way home from work, he and his wife were shotgunned to death as they walked across an open courtyard to their apartment. The first shotgun blast hit Dubeck in the back; the second hit his wife in the face as she turned toward him. Federal investigators said it had been common knowledge in the Las Vegas underworld that there had been at least two organized crime contracts for Dubeck's murder ever since he appeared before the grand jury in the gambling case.

But Calaway's indictment and Dubeck's murder were still a year or so away when the Orange County stock trial ended, at last bringing the Levy caper to a conclusion. The investigation and plea-bargaining and trials in the stock and jewelry cases had stretched out over more than a year, and when Levy was finally sentenced to prison, he was permitted thirty days to put his affairs in order before reporting for incarceration. He couldn't wait thirty days. After three weeks, he called his attorney:

"I want to go now, Michael. I'm going crazy with the waiting. I don't want to wait another week. Tell them to take me now."

On February 26, 1973—the day before his forty-first birthday and eighteen months after his arrest—Alan Levy went to jail.

Epilogue

D espite the long, drawn-out legal proceedings in both the
stock and jewelry cases, the Orange County case was
still in progress when Levy went to jail. Rather than send
him to the federal penitentiary at Terminal Island—twenty-
five miles south of downtown Los Angeles, where most
federal prisoners are held—it was decided to keep him in
a minimum-security Orange County jail known as Theo
Lacey. That way, Orange County authorities figured, when
he was needed as a witness in their trial, he could be
brought to court in a matter of minutes.

"Theo Lacey," Levy says, "wasn't a jail, it was Boys
Town. All that was missing was Father Flanagan, and they
had a guard there named Spencer who could have doubled
for him. I even called him Father Flanagan. Jail? It was a
home for wayward boys. They had two hundred inmates
—mostly chronic drunks, a bunch of young kids on dope,
some husbands who weren't supporting their ex-wives and
maybe four genuine criminals. Criminals? Outside of me,
the biggest crook in the place stole eighteen dollars in a
service station stickup.

"We had barracks inspection every day. Your bed had
to be made just so, and your clothes had to be arranged
in a certain order in this small, wooden box next to the

bed. If you didn't pass inspection, you got a 'gig.' Three
'gigs' and you'd lose your Sunday visits from your friends
and family.

"Right away, I knew I wasn't getting no gigs," Levy
says. "I had a trustee show me how to make my bunk and
I never touched it after that. I slept on top of the covers
every night, and just smoothed it out in the morning.
My clothes? I put them in the box and never touched them
again either. I made friends with a guy in the uniform
room, and he gave me an extra set of everything. I turned
that in for another set when it was dirty, and kept on doing that. I never messed with the original stuff I put in the
box."

On Levy's first morning in prison, he was told to report to Deputy Spencer—"Father Flanagan"—for his work
assignment.

"What did you do on the outside?" Spencer asked him.
"I stole."

"Don't get smart, Levy. Be serious. What did you do?"
"I was a salesman."

"Okay. Come with me."

Spencer took him to the jail kitchen. Levy was puzzled.
"What am I supposed to do here—sell pots and pans to the
other inmates?"

Spencer asked him if he could type.
"No."

"Can you make a salad?"
"No."

"Good, you wash dishes."

Levy's first day in the kitchen went well. The kitchen
crew ate first—and best. They also got their fill of the one
big treat available at Theo Lacey—Kool Aid.

"Can you believe that?" Levy asks, still incredulous. "I'm
in jail and I got a bunch of kids around me who think it's
a big fucking deal to get a free cup of Kool-Aid. Christ . . ."

Levy quickly made friends with the jailhouse medic,

who showed him how to mix mineral oil and iodine into a reasonably tolerable substitute for suntan lotion. When he wasn't working—first in the kitchen, then the library, then the sports locker—Levy often lay in the prison yard, sunning himself.

But he rather enjoyed his job in the sports locker.

"I had charge of checking out all the sports equipment," he says. "We had just about everything there—softball, horseshoes, volleyball, handball, croquet, basketball, ringtoss, badminton, football. I had my own office. It was a great deal, the best job in the whole place."

Still, Levy spent much of his jail-time sleeping. It helped make the days pass more quickly. Sunday was the only day he didn't want to pass quickly. Sunday was visiting day, and he tried to savor every minute of it. Friends came by regularly. So did his attorney, Michael Nasatir. Stan Greenberg, one of the prosecutors who helped put him in jail, also came by to visit him. But Levy's most frequent—and most welcome—visitor was Leesa Cuccinello, an intelligent, voluptuous and utterly delightful girl with a lush, magnificent body, lustrous brown hair that hangs to her waist and a face both beautiful and mature beyond her then-seventeen years.

Leesa was the daughter of a businessman Levy had been involved with briefly between the time of his arrest and his imprisonment. Leesa's father had lost a considerable sum of money in the deal, but she and Levy had fallen in love with each other. She wrote him every day of his confinement and visited him every Sunday, and the hours they spent together passed all too quickly for both of them.

Late in his stay at Theo Lacey, Levy heard that Leonard Bernstein—imprisoned in another correctional facility, up the California coast—was getting out nine days early. Levy asked his attorney, Michael Nasatir, to see if he were also eligible for early release. On March 16—ten days before his ninety days would be up—he received a telegram from

Leesa saying that Nasatir had arranged for him to be released the next day.

At six o'clock the next morning, eighty-one days after Levy was first incarcerated, Leesa was waiting for him at the front gate of the prison, next door to the Orange County dog pound.

In eight months, they would be married—wife No. 7 for him, husband No. 1 for her—but all Levy could think about that morning was how good he felt.

His long hours in the sun, bathed in iodine and mineral oil, had left him as suntanned as a tourist returning home after two weeks in Bermuda or Palm Springs. His refusal to eat all the starchy prison foods had enabled him to lose twenty-eight pounds and six inches off his waist. Bronzed, slimmed down, eager to embrace Leesa, Nicole and freedom, he felt, he told Leesa that day, "like a million dollars."

"In fact," he said, "make that two million dollars. See, I got this plan . . ."

Postscript

The following names appearing in this book are pseudo-nyms and bear no resemblance to any persons living or dead with those names:

Jack Lane, Rod, Tom Wilson, Fats Jackson, Frank, Ludwig Hellmer, Assad, Linda, Tony Bruno, the Baron.